Through the Eyes of Aliens

of related interest

The Passionate Mind
How People with Autism Learn
Wendy Lawson
ISBN 978 1 84905 121 7

Autism and Me DVD
Rory Hoy
ISBN 978 1 84310 546 6

Siblings and Autism
Stories Spanning Generations and Cultures
Edited by Debra L. Cumberland and Bruce E. Mills
ISBN 978 1 84905 831 5

From Isolation to Intimacy
Making Friends without Words
Phoebe Caldwell with Jane Horwood
ISBN 978 1 84310 500 8

Using Intensive Interaction and Sensory Integration
A Handbook for Those who Support People with Severe Autistic Spectrum Disorder
Phoebe Caldwell with Jane Horwood
ISBN 978 1 84310 626 5

Using Intensive Interaction with a Person with a Social or Communicative Impairment
Graham Firth and Mark Barber
ISBN 978 1 84905 109 5

Promoting Social Interaction for Individuals with Communicative Impairments
Making Contact
Edited by M. Suzanne Zeedyk
ISBN 978 1 84310 539 8

Through the Eyes of Aliens

A Book about Autistic People

Jasmine Lee O'Neill

Jessica Kingsley Publishers
London and Philadelphia

First published in the United Kingdom in 1999 by
Jessica Kingsley Publishers Ltd
116 Pentonville Road
London N1 9JB, England
and
400 Market Street, Suite 400
Philadelphia, PA 19106, USA

www.jkp.com

Copyright © 1999 Jasmine Lee O'Neill
Printed digitally since 2011

Library of Congress Cataloging in Publication Data
A CIP catalog record for this book is available from the Library of Congress

British Library Cataloguing in Publication Data
O'Neill, Jasmine Lee
Through the eyes of aliens
1. Autism
I. Title
616.8'982

ISBN 978 1 85302 710 9

For my very wonderful, dear friend,
who breathed air into my dreams so they could take wing;
Whose honest friendship sustained me through aching days;
Whose gentle love coaxed me to bloom like an iris in his
garden;
Whose welcoming heart cherishes misfits,
kind and wise like a peaceful lion:
Bertram A. Ruttenberg, M.D.
You are most beloved.

Contents

§

For an Autistic Child

To you in your world,
Locked inside yourself,
An island,
Isolated winds in your mind,
To you, locked inside beauty,
Inside anguish, inside joy,
You live
Breathe
Die
Emotions
too profound to understand,
Little one curled up rocking,
Your floor your world,
Safe,
Just you,
Your little expressive hands,
Like tiny birds,
talking in flutters,
your little angry snarls
repel a monstrous outside realm,
your beloved treasures:
Buttons
Diminutive faery animals
Smooth wooden beads
Dots of sunlight on your wall
Humming your songs
to calm your anxious hands,

Safe,
Just you,
At one with rhythm,
Your world
only bits of those others
who come and go like currents of air,
barely ruffling your forelock,
Your face a delicate empty mask
to those who see only with eyes,
Those who don't understand
your world,
To me,
watching you,
I see myself,
I sing songs for you,
little one, to tell you
You don't have to forsake your world to be free.

§

ONE

Introducing Autism

There is a huge mob of books on Autism available presently. They attempt to explain this mysterious, unusual, potentially beautiful type of personality. To search for a definition of *Autism* in a dictionary is foolish. The definition will be incomplete and almost always negative. Most often a dictionary won't even point out that Autism is a medical condition, that it is a special kind of mind. Some older dictionaries even insist that it is characterized by delusions, hallucinations, and dull intelligence: all three are totally incorrect.

To more thoroughly understand or appreciate this fascinating human phenomenon, it's necessary to read at least several good books on the subject. It is also very beneficial to view videos of autistic grown-ups and children doing what they naturally do. Even after extensive research, I believe that it is impossible to understand everything. There are several reasons for this:

1. Each autistic individual is different from every other. Each has her or his own fears, joys; each gets excited by different self-stimulating activities. Of course, many of these activities are shared generally among most people with Autism.

2. Autism is a condition of a certain form of isolation. It is always characterized by some type of self-absorption, as well as social and language difficulties or eccentricities. So, even though every person with the condition is unique, there must still be some specific traits (I say 'traits' rather than 'symptoms'; as a term 'symptom' suggests illness. Autism is not an illness) observed in order for the child or adult to be formally diagnosed as being autistic. So, going right along with the characteristic withdrawal and keen self-absorption,

is a closed personality. Some autistics can't reveal deep stirrings within them. Some autistics won't reveal them. Sometimes there is a combination. Since the very private, personal self always remains concealed in some ways, the person stays a mystery. The outside realm doesn't get to see the entirety. There is nothing wrong with that.

3. People who are not autistic lead very different lives from people who are autistic. In Autism, there is a specific brain difference, which influences certain ways of thinking. Although the author of this text has done research into this concept, it isn't the purpose of this book to discuss neurology. Certain limitations and gifts of the autistic brain separate the autistic person from the non-autistic majority. People who are not autistic can't possibly become autistic enough truly to comprehend what a life with Autism is like. However, they can simulate some autistic sensory experiences. They can also grow to appreciate a lot by using imagination, caring, and having an open mind.

4. Too many parents and caregivers of autistics believe written or spoken misconceptions. The word of a physician or psychologist need not be law. Some so-called experts are incompetent. A desperate parent can eat up everything a sneaky physician says. Some of the autistic behaviour explained by outsiders is speculation. Sometimes there are no answers available. Care must be taken to consult with a reputable, experienced Autism specialist, not only a general practitioner, or a paediatrician. Even when the best specialist is involved, there won't be answers for everything. So that is the reason total understanding may be elusive. Autism is indeed complicated.

To understand and appreciate uniqueness should be the foremost goal of the parent, friend, or caregiver of the autistic person. Careful, interested research will yield results. Combining medical texts with other sources is a very fine way to go about personal study.

The most helpful approach to understanding Autism is to meet autistic people, themselves. Read their poems, letters or essays; attend their speeches; look at their sculpture or paintings; listen to their voices; question them; show them respect; learn from them; observe their way of living.

The purpose of this book is to educate. I am autistic. I have gained extensive experience simply by living with fairly severe Autism for my lifetime. I will present my views in this book as an aid to those who are interested.

My goal is to show that Autism can be seen as a truly beautiful event. It is quite tiring to read book after book denouncing Autism as a horrible condition. I am qualified to offer an opposite opinion. The theme of this book is to say that difference can be wonderful, and Autism shouldn't be tampered with, or altered. Autistic people shouldn't be changed. They shouldn't be banished, ridiculed, or forced to act as anyone other than who they are, naturally. Autistic people have the same rights as others.

Throughout history, autistics have been denied human rights to dignity. The root of the word Autism is *auto*, which simply means *self*. Yet the treatment these individuals have got creates a dismal portrait... as though the root word perhaps means *ogre* or *idiot* or *worthless*.

Autistic people are often victims of oppression. They are often discriminated against in the same manner as people of various colours or religions are discriminated against. One form of discrimination doesn't differ from another. Discrimination is all bad and very wrong.

Autistic people are innately separate and different. But they are human beings. They just live their own lives in an interesting, unusual fashion.

In this text, I shall illustrate many of the ways of autistic people. I hope I will be able to increase the understanding of the outside, big world, as I call it, as I stay enclosed within my own autistic world. It is definitely not my wish to lose my Autism or to 'emerge from Autism'. That is a foolish phrase, anyway, invented by non-autistics! It is a goal to education, to create fresh pathways. An autistic should be proud of who he or she is. Great fortitude can come from being autistic. Autistics can be coached so they will be able to use the special gifts they have. They are not incomplete or less than others.

Ever since the term *Autism* was used formally to describe a specific group of children by Leo Kanner in 1943, the condition has been misunderstood. Research has proven wrong the theory that parents cause their child's behaviour. The public has been told that Autism was purely emotional. In the 1960s and 1970s, autistic children were considered to be seriously emotionally disturbed. Therapies addressed that concern. More recently, researchers banished that hypothesis. They presented the idea of an organic cause of Autism, saying it has just about nothing to do with the emotions. In my opinion, Autism is organic as well as emotional. A brain difference can affect emotions. The organic function of the brain is the core. That, in turn, alters emotions and sensory experiences.

Autism does affect all aspects of a person. It needs to be addressed as a global condition. It needs to be seen as multi-faceted. An autistic world is fragmented. Oft times the fragments seem disjointed. They are all part of the whole person. An autistic individual may appear simultaneously complex and simple. Simple doesn't mean stupid. Judging an individual with Autism with ordinary person terms doesn't accurately describe the individual. Definitions fall short.

The common images of autistic children are fairly familiar. They include scenes of children happily sitting quiet, rocking their bodies, and scenes of mute children banging their chins with their palms. Behind these images are flowing complex thoughts and emotions. These various scenes will be dealt with in a later chapter. By making the effort to identify the child's reasons for behaviour, a large leap is taken towards understanding.

The goal of understanding must not be to punish or reform the child. It must be to learn to love purely, and to nurture that precious, unique, individual spirit hiding within the autistic person. The person must be allowed to remain autistic. It is born into him, and is lifelong. There are no cures, nor should there be.

I believe that is why Autism has eluded science and baffled physicians. I believe Autism is a marvellous occurrence of nature, not a tragic example of the human mind gone wrong. In many cases, Autism also can be a kind of genius undiscovered.

Autistic people are worth getting to know. They are valuable just as they are. They can display innovative thinking. Many times they use language in a delightful fashion, such as the young man who referred to a hole in his sock as a 'temporary loss of knitting'. We autistics all have our individual small quirks. These are strong parts of our personalities. This is some of what makes us who we are.

The best way for me to describe Autism is to use my own colourful autistic language. As I stated before, the non-autistic can gain much by using imagination. It is probably much easier for a non-autistic to try to imagine how it might feel to live as an autistic than it is the reverse.

Autism isn't confined to a certain type of human being. There are many types. Autism never manifests itself in the same way twice. The discussions in this book cover all, and the text uses Autism as a simple term to encompass all the terms used on the autistic continuum. These include Kanner Syndrome Autism, Asperger Syndrome, Pervasive Developmental Disorder, and even various types of dyslexics, hyperlexics, and schizoid personalities (although true schizophrenia is *not* Autism).

An individual who is autistic may also have two or more of these combined. For an example, I am a classical Kanner autistic also with Asperger Syndrome traits. I fit every one of the criteria diagnosing what is now called Autistic Disorder, as well as some criteria diagnosing Asperger Syndrome. Basically, as a poet, writer, painter, illustrator, and musician, I am more creative than the average autistic, and that comes from Asperger Syndrome.

I do have very typically autistic limits and have autistic thought behaviour, and I do exhibit communication difficulties, and severe social difference, and am withdrawn.

It is a myth that severely autistic people are all retarded, mentally. Actually, some people with severe Autism are brilliant. Also, a single individual can show both low-functioning and high-functioning in different areas.

It takes time and care to assess and know each person with Autism. Each is a complicated, wondrous being, so it's a terrible injustice to hastily label an autistic person, then consider her or him too feeble to have a real life.

There, indeed, lies a lot beyond those so-called empty autistic eyes.

§

The Autistic World

The world of an autistic person is not stagnant. Things are constantly going on in the closed, wee, bubble of an autistic person's consciousness. There are so many things to taste, to smell, to hear. It often seems like a crazy puzzle. It is a deeply sensory world. Tiniest details are usually filed away in the brain and remembered to be brought forth at will and re-experienced.

Sometimes the concept of time has no meaning. To the autistic person, time can seem completely different than to a non-autistic person. It helps to be very specific with time. It is true that some autistic behaviours can disappear with growing older. However, more often, they change into other behaviours as the autistic teenager or young adult experiences new events.

There are no miracle cures. There are a few extremely rare cases written about where a person's Autism seems to vanish – a spontaneous recovery. I am very skeptical of those reports. Most likely, the person never was truly autistic in the first place. Or, some of the noticeable behaviours could have tapered off, so those who know the adult or child well say she no longer seems autistic.

Yet Autism is very holistic in its manifestation. Much of it is inward and unable to be seen or proven by others. People say that the autistic person has improved if she behaves more like those surrounding her. Or people hope she may be losing her Autism.

As Autism is a physical brain difference, it is lifelong. One cannot get a brain transplant, so there is only so much to do that may make the condition seem less noticeable, and in some cases, that doesn't work much at all. Actually, it's unfortunate that parents, schoolteachers, doctors, and others even want to mold autistic people into something they're not. Trying to make your autistic child seem less autistic is to admit you're not happy with her as she is. That can be very devastating to the child.

The autistic world isn't a dark and horrid chamber. It perhaps sometimes appears that way to outsiders. Knowledge and understanding will lessen the fear. For, as an autistic fears new or unknown people, events, places, even foods, a non-autistic may also fear a world inside another that seems incomprehensible.

The inside home of an autistic can feel like a safe refuge. Autistics are extreme examples of people who just need to be more cloistered. Not all are shy, but all do need to feel the calm of their inner experiences. It centres and soothes some of the anxiety that comes from outside confusion. It's comforting to know that you have a portable sanctuary.

Of course there is no visible bubble that encapsulates autistic people's bodies. The separate, little worlds of autistic people are made up of individual, vivid experiences, sensory stimulations, and the ways that individual interprets his environment. These private worlds can be very tiny or very big. An outside person never truly knows what's going on inside another's mind.

The apparent isolation of the autistic child is often a secondary happening caused by the fundamental differences in the brain. These differences don't result in an illness with a treatment, or an imbalance corrected by drugs.

Many children with Autism are gleeful when they are alone, absorbed tightly into themselves. They may giggle, or express other emotions loudly or quietly. They can often feel quite content.

I do not believe that a true autistic ever comes out of himself. There is always some degree of staying within. Even when he answers a question, he can still be pretty much inside himself. He is operating from a spot at his deepest centre. Sometimes autistics are oblivious to certain occurrences outside themselves. Other times they are hyper-aware, only they simply don't respond to sights or sounds in the regular way. This shouldn't be treated as a bad thing.

To most autistics, their own worlds are more familiar and preferable to the outside big world. An autistic infant will appear uninterested in the surrounding environment. She will explore only those things immediately available to her, usually parts of her own body. Parents frequently report long spans of silence or screaming in their unusual baby.

Professionals in the child behaviour field have claimed that all babies go through an 'autistic' phase in early development. That is no longer said. (In that case, the world 'autistic' was used as an adjective that is separate from the condition known as 'Autism'. The term 'autistic thinking' is used to describe one whose thoughts are strongly centred on the self.)

Actually, regular babies become interested in their environment almost immediately and do respond to it in their baby ways. Autism isn't always apparent in the earliest months of the child. Yet a lot of parents report that their child appeared odd from birth. A large percentage of autistic infants begin their rocking at the age of only a few months, and they rock in their cribs for long periods, often laughing.

Since the inner world of the autistic is something one is born with, it would be terrible to try to take it away. Even in those children who don't show signs of their Autism until after age two or three, the seed of Autism has alrealcy been planted in them since before birth. No event of trauma after birth causes Autism. Symptoms of Post-traumatic stress disorder can mimic some traits in Autism. But a

child can't become autistic (only perhaps 'autistic-like') upon witnessing an awful car crash, or a parent killed.

Many texts paint a colourless portrait of the autistic world. It seems most people view it as dismal grey, as a dungeon without windows. To me, it is a rainbow prism. It can be a world of bright fragments, like stained glass. It is a place which many children don't wish to leave. It is a home. It is a way of life. Most autistics are unforgettable. Rather than seeing them with pity or fear, try to wonder about them. What a fascinating realm to study!

What is really so hideous about bubble children, or children in boxes? There can be a few traits of Autism which become terrifying to the one looking on. Behind those actions, though, are reasons and motives that create the behaviour. So, before condemning, do try to discover the reasons. Try to stand in the doorway of the autistic world. You may not be allowed to enter the domain of an autistic individual fully. But you can get a glimpse of what goes on.

The autistic individual certainly has the right to this special home within. It is not a dream world as some dictionaries imply. It's not a spot in the mind filled with hallucinations. Rather, the person sees what is around him with extra-acute sight. An autistic observing the outside world experiences it as surreal, not as a made-up work of art in the mind.

Often, autistic children and grown-ups are described by big-worlders as being 'spaced out' or 'in another world'. The latter description is sort of true. Yet it's actually described more accurately by saying the autistic is 'blocking out the outside world' or 'focusing and turning within".

The autistic brain functions in a way that means that autistics can focus attention like a laser beam, excluding most other stimuli. At the same time, this type of brain has a different way of orienting to various stimuli, so the individual may strongly react to a tiny sound that nobody else can hear. Or the individual may be unable to tune out background noise that is a mere hum to everyone else.

An autistic person can become absorbed in the motion of wind tossed trees, or in a dot of sunlight on the wall. This can give an illusion of being 'spaced out'. Many times the eyes appear to be looking in, not out. Complex images or thoughts can be flashing through the mind behind those so-called vacant eyes. On the contrary, the eyes of an autistic most definitely are not vacant. They are deep. As many autistics don't make much contact with the eyes of other people, this could lead to others saying such things.

Too much guessing about the inner worlds leads to a portrait of negativity. It also strips the autistic's true self away, because outsiders are too busy projecting their own speculations and personalities onto that person.

You can't judge the world of another as inferior, because you don't live in that world. Each human being has a personal collection of experiences. A person's family and house may be his whole universe in his perception. An autistic perception is just different from other perceptions.

The autistic world is comfortable. It is a safe place to ground oneself in. Autistic children can keep their inner sanctuaries, as well as grow and learn, and become educated.

Their worlds can expand to include fresh experiences. I think it is a very bad idea to try to force one's way into an autistic's world. That is a grave threat to the autistic person. It is an overwhelming assault to the special one's tender senses. All things coming from the outside must be gentle, sometimes devoid of emotion, so as not to overwhelm.

Different autistics have sensitivities in different areas, and sometimes combinations of these. The inner world is a way for the individual to feel grounded. It gives private fortitude. It can comfort when the surrounding environment seems to be erupting in chaos. It must be remembered that, just as the person with Autism is in many ways handicapped in the outside, big world, the person of the big world is also in many ways handicapped in the autistic world.

You should not seek to change what you are, or try to do it to another. I also don't agree with the therapists who try to prevent an autistic child from seeking refuge in her inner world. There are extroverts and introverts. If an autistic person doesn't actively relate the way others do, so what?

Since there is so much beneath the surface of someone who has Autism, the person actually is probably absorbing more than it appears. The child or adult can be both oblivious and hyper-aware, de-

pending on circumstances. So assessment of someone at a glance isn't
sufficient.

Good professionals in the field spend a lot of time getting to know
each new autistic client or pupil. They respect that sensitive person's
characteristic to live like a shy sea creature inside a vibrant, colourful,
self-containing shell home. They are interested in each one as a human being. They delight in the surprises that unfold as they get to
know the autistic individual.

The pathway to appreciating each one can be travelled by doctors,
teachers, therapists, psychologists, parents, siblings, and friends –
even strangers who have a fire to learn about others.

By stepping into a new dimension of thought and experience, you
can educate yourself. You can have fresh insights. You can be enriched.

Stepping into the following chapters will begin a journey towards
understanding.

§

THREE

Autism and Sense Organs

Parents of autistic children report that often their child acts deaf or blind. They will describe the child ignoring loud abrupt noises, but quickly responding to interesting tiny sounds such as a candy wrapper being torn. There are cases where a person is both truly deaf and autistic, just as there are cases of Autism combined with Rett Syndrome (which occurs only in mentally retarded girls), or some types of seizures.

The sensory experiences of an autistic person play a huge role in the condition. Extensive research in this area reveals that there is only rarely a physical abnormality of any of the sense organs of an autistic child. Yet these children do react eccentrically to sensory stimuli. Oft times information being processed into the brain from a sensory stimulus will even cause the child or adult to react in panic or rage in a big way.

Autistic people live in a keenly sensory world. Their self-stimulatory behaviours are all connected with senses. This chapter will point out that it is exciting and a thing of beauty to be gifted with unusual sensory opportunities. Sometimes being hypersensitive to something can cause emotional or physical pain. But it is also incredible and deeply human to experience profoundly acute emotions and sensory occurrences, even if some people do refer to this as being 'primitive'. Intense emotions are essential to creating tremendous works of art. Sometimes depression or mental torments are partners of genius, but not in all cases. Yet, if one has a capacity to feel total exaltation, the capacity is also there to feel anguish. Senses can dramatically affect emotions, of course. This fact is very evident in autistic people.

Some senses can be heightened; others dulled in the same child. Several professionals have stated they believe autistic self-stimulating actions to be a desperate way of communication. They feel that the child is distressed by one or more abnormal sense organs, so she attempts to normalize the channels by engaging in repetitive activities. It is sometimes claimed that the so-called Autism disappears or lessens once therapy is begun to bring the upset sensory channel in line with the other ones.

That theory is too limiting. It doesn't take into account the differences of the autistic brain. Sensory organs have nothing to do with autistic metabolism or the various chemical syntheses going on in the brain. To research that particular subject, there are several looks listed at the close of this book.

Theories to define Autism come and go. Autistic behaviour and living as an autistic does not change when new revolutionary research results are published. One doctor or one new trend isn't enough to form a whole picture of this condition, Autism. So many times the human aspect is neglected.

Autistic people aren't specimens. They're not machines or cars to be tinkered with until they perform exactly the way you want them to. Although they are difficult to understand, they are humans, with amazing, special characteristics and even gifts.

Autistic persons become quite self-absorbed. That doesn't mean they are mentally selfish. It means they are deeply concerned about their bodies and what's happening to them. They are deeply submerged within themselves. So it is very difficult to look outward. Sometimes they perceive objects as parts of themselves.

I am both hyper-emotional and hyper-sensory. To me, everything is acutely heightened, and I also have extremely intense emotions. All of my senses are finely tuned. Some other people with Autism have only two or so senses which are very acute.

Many times, sensory stimuli are perceived in fragments. The child focuses on one sense, such as sight. Whilst he is examining something with his vision, he sees every minute detail and colours are vibrant, perhaps radiatingly brilliant like the jewel tones of a modern painting. As he brings in the visual stimulus, however, he loses track of his other senses. So he doesn't make much sense of sounds in the background. Also his body seems suspended, floating, as he loses knowledge of feeling touch. Being able to focus on only one or two things at a time is not a sign of low intelligence. It's simply a brain that zeroes in rather than zeroes out. It is rather a purer way of thinking that has advantages. Autistic people aren't jugglers of information, so it is easier for them to be overloaded.

A large number of autistics have keen hearing. Not only can they detect sounds that are out of the regular person's range; they react to specific sounds in ways others don't. To an autistic child, that rustling candy wrapper can pierce the air. The child recognizes that there are goodies inside candy wrappers and investigates! Yet the child may not stir if a sudden sound bursts nearby him. The loud sound disturbs him and hurts his ears more than the unfurling candy wrapper. So he blocks it out. This is selective deafness.

Depending upon the tone, pitch or quality of sound, it can cause very strong reactions. Autistics can take advantage of sound, as well, to comfort themselves. Music is the best example of this. It seems born into nearly every person with Autism to love music. Music is a powerful thing, indeed. It can be used as a non-verbal language. The heavenly combination of melody and rhythm envelops the tender autistic child and brings joyful calm. Conversations with music can take place. In music therapy, a trained professional communicates with the child by matching the child's moods with improvised tunes. Soon the child can learn to influence the music's feeling with his own. He can participate in and initiate a conversation in a way that doesn't threaten him or transform him into somebody else.

Besides music, other sounds can bring a peaceful inner feeling. A lot of autistics make small sounds to themselves. In those who speak, they often will talk to themselves, chatting away about almost anything, and echoing tunes, phrases, or words that sound pleasing to them. The sounds of certain words can roll about deliciously and provide auditory stimulation. Even in completely non-verbal autistics there is a rare child who makes no sound at all. Each child picks and utters key noises to himself. Sometimes he murmurs and hums along with rocking his body. Repeating sound patterns is comforting. It also simply feels nice. Other people do things that simply feel very good. Why shouldn't an autistic do that as well? Saying autistics have weird behaviour and are so hard to understand and get close to is not a good enough reason.

Sometimes the voices of other persons can be unbearable to an autistic. Sometimes there is a certain tone quality that can't be tolerated, such as a high, gratey voice. To imagine its effect, think of a sound you don't like: perhaps long fingernails on a blackboard. In your mind listen to that dragging of those awful fingernails down a blackboard: Screeee! An autistic person will react strongly to a noise that affects her in the same way. A barking dog or jangling phone can be devastating. Also, many conversations going on at once will become a confusing blur, as the person with Autism can't process them to decipher their meaning. When only one voice is speaking, the autistic one generally won't have a problem grasping content. This isn't to suggest that the non-autistic person should speak extra slowly and loudly. That is an insult to the autistic listener's intelligence. Do speak clearly, however, and make sure the autistic person knows you're addressing her. Autistics often avoid eye contact, so don't assume you're being ignored or treated rudely, if you're not looked at directly.

Autistic people often glance out of the sides of their eyes at objects or other people. They have very acute peripheral vision and a memory for details that others miss. Gazing directly at people or animals is many times too overwhelming for the autistic one. Eyes are very intense and show emotions. It can feel creepy to be searched with the eyes. Some autistic people don't even look at the eyes of actors or news reporters on television. Eye contact must never be forced! Colours seem brilliant, radiating. Patterns and lights fascinate many autistic people. When looking at a painting, it can seem as though the image is enveloping and drawing in the viewer. This can happen with a non-autistic person, too. The autistic person will feel the object with her whole being. A painting becomes entire body stimulus. The colours can practically be tasted, the rhythm of the brushstrokes can be heard; the paint can be smelled. To the autistic individual, a painting or sculpture asks to be touched. It's an experience that must be devoured. It must be explored totally. It's a lovely thing to participate in something so fully, although of course museum guards do tend to get upset if somebody tries to taste or touch the artwork. Some outdoor sculpture gardens have pieces that may be touched. The growing child with Autism would probably be very happy to be able to benefit from such an outing. Everyone can enjoy art, even if the enjoyment is on different levels.

Outlines of objects can stand out sharply. Sometimes there are also perception difficulties. Because autistic people are concerned with the space immediately surrounding their bodies, they tend to prefer their proximal senses: touch, taste, smell, to their distal senses: sight, hearing. However, that doesn't mean that sight and hearing can't be also developed to unusually high levels. I am one of those autistics whose every sense is very highly developed.

Being able to focus on small details, an autistic person generally takes in parts of a whole. They become pre-occupied with fragments. A child may be interested in a certain book, not for its content, but because it has a fancy velour cover with shining golden stamping. Anything sparkly or glowing attracts the autistic attention.

Autistic people get obsessed with specific objects for their own reasons. The reasons can vary from person to person. Some people are willing and capable of telling you why they are interested in something. Questions should be asked of them, never demanded. Asking a direct question can be yet another sensory overload to a sensitive person. Questions should be asked because you are caring and curious. The finest Autism specialists are those who are interested in knowing their clients as unique beings, not as specimens. That should also be the motive for the parent of an autistic child.

There is not really going to be an autistic child who completely and constantly is oblivious to absolutely everything. There is bound to be a spark that will evoke a response connected to one of the sensory organs. As all autistic people do stay to some degree within themselves, it's not correct to assume that the apparently most severely withdrawn child is also mentally retarded. Shutting out is a sensory response. Just as the sense organs can be very acute, they can also appear to be underdeveloped. The same child can have one sense overdeveloped, and another underdeveloped.

Therapies can help to desensitize the over acute sense, as well as increase the one considered to be deficient. This may not be a wise idea always. When you tamper with something someone has been given, it's not always for the good. Unless the autistic individual is showing distress very often concerning too sensitive senses, it's best to leave nature alone. I, myself, love all of my senses, and cherish the profound experiences they bring to my life. They fuel creativity as well as provide a lovely feeling to me. Even in non-creative autistic individuals, the same feelings are useful because they give pleasure.

Much of the autistic world is made of experiences from the senses, as well as mistrust or fear of what is in the outside big world. In sensory and emotional stimulus, autistics resemble animals. Animals rely heavily upon their senses to give them information about their environment. Animals are not stupid or unthinking; they simply have brains that function differently from human brains. Also, in some ways, both types of brains function the same. Autistic children are on another level of consciousness. Just because they rely on their senses, and their emotional responses might be more primitive doesn't make them a lesser kind of human, just as it doesn't make the animals less. Man is an animal too, it should be remembered.

Basically, an autistic person regards her environment the same way as an animal. There is a strong fear response built in that is easily activated by a powerful sensory stimulus. A loud noise may send an autistic scurrying in panic. Non-autistics don't understand that type of reaction. They haven't had to live with this type of fear. Try to imagine that something you consider startling has frightened you abruptly. Try to be patient with the child of Autism whose reactions seem to be puzzling. There is always a reason for the reaction. The reason may not be easily discovered, but it's not some made-up delusion.

Autistic people are very close to their senses. There are countless sensory delights that fascinate them which seem to be overlooked or undetected by regulars. So many things seem wonderful. They explore their environment as though noticing it for the first time. With a child's joy and interest in simple things, the autistic person records sensory impressions: the smell of melting candles, rice cooking, new magazines, the feel of velvet and marble, the taste of smooth, satiny wood, the pit-pat of bare feet on tiles, the look of clouds gliding high, the feel of a horse's nose, the chalky taste of seashells.

Sensory channels can also get confused so the autistic receives muffled signals or scrambled information. That can be frightening, yet also intriguing. It's probably more alarming to the child who doesn't have a good grasp of language. It is possible, in this scrambly way, not only to see colours, but almost to smell them, too. It's like getting a complete impression of a fragment of information.

One sense is never enough! Autistic people like to explore with more than one sense. Think of a cat, who gracefully approaches a piece of furniture, sniffs it, then rubs her body against it. Sometimes she even tastes it. Then she decides what to make of her accumulated sensory information. Actually, cats show many autistic-like traits.

Many children or adults with Autism also sniff people and objects, one of their ways to explore and decipher.

Autistics usually are quite picky about foods. As eating incorporates taste, touch, smell and sight, it can become quite an interesting experience. Most autistic people like food. Meal times become part of their daily routines. They may get fixated on one or two specific foods for a time period. Getting them to try other foods can be extremely difficult. It can also be traumatic to them. They may have trouble recognizing other foods as edible. Since they live by specifics, not generalizations, it may be necessary to help them to discover that there are a huge variety of goodies for them to enjoy.

To ensure that the child gets correctly nourished, give a daily multi-vitamin, multi-mineral complex. When trying to introduce new foods, do so patiently, one at a time. Remember that the child with Autism is going to react the same way as do most children who wrinkle their noses at the tiny green forest of broccoli on their plates and whine, 'Yuk!' Only, a child with Autism's reaction will probably be more severe. It's important to begin introducing new foods early, so the child doesn't get hooked on one food for years, and suffer malnutrition. Always be caring when helping an extra-finicky child explore new culinary delights. Never force him to eat something. You will only lessen his trust in you, and frighten him. It is completely *essential* that your autistic child trusts you. Also, if a child is made to eat something by force, it may cause a tantrum – or perhaps you will find the newly-swallowed food simply spat back up on the table. Autistic people can be extraordinarily stubborn! Actually, they are definitely not easy to care for. But they are what they are.

Their reasons for avoiding a food may not seem evident at first. Try to discover why. Fear could be one big reason. Autistics avoid change and are afraid of new things. So instead of trying to stomp out the Autism itself, which is impossible, be aware of its cardinal characteristics. Work with them, not against them. Always remember how sensitive the child is. Sensitivity is really a very lovely thing. If you're not afraid of something that doesn't mean your child also is not afraid of it. Fears that seem small to the big world people can be consuming to an autistic child or grown-up. If you were terrified of spiders, how would you feel if someone you trust places an immense tarantula upon your lunch plate? A small autistic child may be afraid of a specific colour, perhaps coppery-orange. He's going to react with great distress, therefore, when he sees a pile of carrots on his platter! Autistic people are famous for eccentric eating habits!

If various gentle methods still don't work, and you still haven't got the child to try that one item of food he seems most against trying, then to hell with that food, and move on. Consider the possibility that he simply hates it just like any other child (and adult) will hate certain foods. An autistic can tell a lot by the scent of something. He may find its texture unpleasant in his mouth, just as some people don't like the natural slimy feeling of cooked okra.

The autistic person has as much right as anybody to enjoy his meals. As the child gets older, he should also be encouraged to participate in preparing foods. Don't overlook him only because he's autistic. Highly-strung children can be deeply hurt by being ignored (even though that seems to be what they prefer usually) whilst attention is doted upon siblings. The autistic child can find fun in helping in the kitchen. If he is wild with a knife, then give him a different task to do, such as folding the napkins. Take advantage of what he picks up quickly and seems to enjoy. He may be very interested in tactile stimulation, and may like smoothing the tablecloth. Even very simple chores can be delightful to the sensitive autistic child. Be sure to praise him often.

Autism is not synonymous with 'idiocy,' or 'inability'. On the contrary, most autistic individuals are able in quite unique ways, and they may not grow as bored with the same chore as a non-autistic child would. Incorporate the chore into the routine. Then the child will look forward to it. Many autistics can even learn to cook.

Giving easy, little tasks such as laundry folding or sandwich making can be first steps toward discovering the hidden intelligence and abilities within your autistic youngster.

Allow him to proceed forward in steps. He will need his own pace to work by, even if it seems too slow for the parent or therapist. I emphasize statements like this because they are profoundly important. Society brainwashes individuals to believe that slow means 'stupid', and that Autism means 'total retard'. The stigma against mentally retarded non-autistics is also inexcusable. They also may have abilities hidden away, along with a special type of intelligence that surrounding humans were simply too ignorant to notice. Intelligence is manifest in various, multiple ways. Society must be aware of this, and start to learn how to observe it. A person who truly is a genius may score poorly on a standard IQ test. Intelligence is even evident in the cells of the body, as they grow, multiply, and perish. Intelligence is alive and vital. Some of the most brilliant people, whose minds are world famous, did badly at school or even left school early.

Intelligence is also present in the sense organs, because intelligence is present throughout an organism, not only in the brain. Learning how each individual autistic person's senses function is one crucial key to understanding that person. The senses of an autistic can seem too acute at some times and not acute enough other times. These particular patterns need patience to observe. The teacher or parent can learn the signs of when the child is reacting to an overwhelming stimulus, or trying to heighten another.

Touch is a major sense with the autistic. Many children are very tactile defensive, and will pull away if a person or animal touches them. Other children are tactile defensive with all except one or a few people they have learnt to trust. When the skin is highly sensitive it feels explosive if another person touches. Nerves will create a sensation as if they are screaming, as if they feel pain. It is a kind of emotional pain. This can also occur with certain fabrics. Autistics will often rub their skin or brush soft fabric against it, or even poke or scratch it. As the skin is the largest organ of the body, it serves as the barrier to keep the big world out there, and the autistic world within its limited boundaries. Touch from another can be very startling and intrusive. The autistic person has personal rules about everything in her world. These rules often contradict the social rules of others. The autistic may not allow touching, or if she does allow it, it will be a certain type that doesn't threaten her. A hello handshake may be seen as a threat. The autistic person should never be forced to shake a hand or hug someone.

During the 1960s and 1970s many so-called therapies were developed to use with autistic children. Some included electroconvulsive shock treatments to attempt to punish the child for displaying an innate trait of Autism, such as avoidance of eye contact, or pulling away from a trained therapist's extended hand. The hypersensitive child of Autism was simply reacting to a stimulus that disturbed her, in the case of the offered hand, or a pat on her head. She was keeping herself intact and safe in her own way. But for doing that, she would be given a 'mild' electric shock. I do not care how mild it is said to be: *All* shock treatments to an autistic person are barbaric. Also, to an already profoundly sensitive child, a so-called mild shock can be registered in her brain as a devastatingly painful attack.

What was often achieved in these therapy programmes was the training of a child to give up out of fear and boredom, and just take the nagging therapist's hand. Teaching by fear never really works. The children may eventually behave the way you want them to. But it is out of fear of you and confusion as to why you're punishing them for avoiding something they find distasteful or even terrifying. You cannot correct fear with more fear. You can only sometimes achieve a result you consider satisfactory but actually isn't. In this case you are merely getting a child to perform like a trained dog in a circus. That is not education.

The shock treatments have been abolished, except in certain institutions that operate largely secretly so the public is kept ignorant of their methods. Shock treatments are an example of how delicate, sensitive people can be brutalized by professionals. Everything affects an autistic individual's senses. If the child is so averse to touching the hand of another person, then forget trying to get her to shake hands with people. If she doesn't ever perform certain social norms, that's not so terrible. She is not like other people.

Some autistics enjoy gentle hugs, or even rolling about on the carpet, being tickled. These, too, are delights of the senses. It is true that the child may be enjoying the sensation itself more than the presence of the person providing the sensation. However, emotions are sensations, too, and autistic people have plenty of emotions.

Even among non-autistics, there are huggy-kissy people, and much more reserved people. There are people who are blind and deaf, and people who are endowed with amazing senses. Sometimes several of these types are combined in a single autistic person. You may observe the same child pressing her hands over her ears to shut out the painful jangling of the telephone, and cranking up the volume of her favourite song on the stereo. Different stimuli affect one person in different ways.

You may observe the same autistic person rubbing sandpaper on his bare arm, or banging his knuckles sharply into a solid wooden dresser, then peering at them as if to say, 'Oh, hello, hand. So you do belong to me, then'. Sometimes the body feels fragmented, also, so it appears to be suspended or floating in pieces. This can be an eerie but neat sensation. A lot of self-stimulations, including rocking the body, swaying, flapping the hands, rubbing the skin, and countless others, are pleasurable, soothing connections with the senses. They help ground the autistic person, provide rhythm and order, calm, and simply feel good!

§

Autism and Emotions

It is a total myth that autistics do not feel or express emotion. Slowly, people begin to realize this. Most parents have always been aware that their child does feel emotion. Many feel emotions in a very big way. The emotions lay at a deeper level within than do the sensory experiences. Sense experiences frequently cause an emotional experience.

In the autistic, it sometimes appears that the senses operate separately from the emotions, sort of disjointed. Outbursts of emotions can occur abruptly, out of air, with no detectable sensory cause. Just the same, an overwhelming sensory occurrence can trigger a tantrum or a flight response. The emotions of an autistic are as complex as the senses. Anyone's emotions are hard to guess. There is much too much guessing involved in situations concerning autistic people. Too many people on the outside make hasty assumptions, 'She feels this way,' or 'He won't mind that'. If someone makes a wrong assumption about me, I get angry.

Even with verbal autistics, it can be hard to communicate feelings effectively. Feeling the deep emotion in a private inside place is quite different from finding an explanation for it that other people will comprehend. Autistic people generally don't seem to feel subtle emotions. Everything happens on a large level. They also often don't feel the same emotions during a particular event that someone else feels.

Despite their odd ways and unique type of alien status, they still need love and caring, and a lot of attention. They often do feel like aliens because others do things they don't understand or feel a need to do. They don't understand much of the big world. The big world doesn't understand the autistic world. Both are largely lost in each other's world. Since neither one can become the other, it is useless to try. Yet, autistics are not the ones abusing non-autistics. It is the other way around. So it is the larger society which needs to appreciate and to understand.

Autistic people don't like to be considered aliens or freaks. Many autistic people like being autistic, and enjoy being different. But they do not like to be wrongly accused of anything, or judged according to textbooks. Their feelings are quite well developed, even if not revealed in all cases.

Emotion was always a confusing issue in the study of Autism. First, Autism was blamed on parents who were said to be uncaring, cold, and unreceptive to the child's needs. People thought the sensitive, hurt child became autistic to protect himself from his unfeeling parents. The mother was especially blamed for this. That theory of unloving 'refrigerator parents' has been proven wrong.

More recently, the child has been blamed for causing his parents' unhappiness. Some parents consider their child unfeeling and think he doesn't love them. They interpret autistic behaviour to be the child rejecting his parents. This theory also is wrong.

Autistic people can feel deep love for others. They can feel deep sadness and ecstasy. They are able to feel the entire rainbow of emotions that exists, including jealousy and envy. They can't always name or define their individual emotions, and the myriad of simultaneous feelings can seem confusing.

There are autistics who do feel tremendously powerful feelings, along with serenity like a still pool. Emotions make one vital and alive, like surging blood in the veins. Superb art is born of amazingly fine-tuned emotion and intellect. Emotions can be devastating, as well. When they go up and down like tidal waves, they can be deeply unsettling.

The chaos of the outside big world is the cause of many outbursts of an autistic person. In the home the atmosphere should be kept peaceful. Autistic people need calmness throughout their lives. When someone is complicated within by nature, any external craziness makes it worse. Autistic children are distractible and need quiet in their learning environments.

Events that others take for granted can bring total glee or despair to an autistic individual. They tend to make mountains out of things others consider rather unimportant. It the daily routine is disrupted, there is one major reason for an overpowering siege of emotions. Out-of-control feelings resemble a herd of wee horses, all charging in opposite directions. The feelings come in waves; tsunamis roiling upward from the spirit's deepest centre. Emotions come with unbelievable force. Parents can do a lot to ease their children's emotion storms with communication and explanation.

It is most comfortable to have emotions that feel balanced, more in a straight line. Too many sham ups and downs are too much to take. It's easy to get overwhelmed in emotion as well as in senses when you're autistic, because you're so sensual.

When planned things don't go the way the autistic thinks, plans, or hopes, disaster can result. The person feels as though everything is crashing in upon her. Routine and rituals (habits) bring comfort. They provide structure and safety and order. Autistics love order. Order is part of their world. So when plans fall apart, it's a personal threat to their world. They are indeed very touchy, easily hurt, easily upset. Anything new, especially an unknown person, does tend to bother them. It is cruel to get angry with an autistic person when she reacts in panic to a disruption. There are no words to describe how it feels to have something taken away from you, for example when something you are counting on gets botched. When someone does not do something he promised to do, no matter what the reason is, it feels as though the person let you down. An autistic understands, fundamentally, only that she feels acute disappointment and often anger. The anger gets directed at the other person in many cases. An autistic person may get very angry with somebody who has to change plans due to illness. It's really not the person's fault he got ill. Yet, despite intellectually knowing that fact, the autistic one's emotions run away with her. Oft times nobody is able to console those wild emotions. The feelings of desperation drown out any self-soothing attempts. As quickly as possible, the painful change must be righted and things restored to be the way they should be, the way the autistic expects them to be.

People with Autism many times express emotion resulting from something inside them. They may laugh at a certain sound or amuse themselves by repeating an action. They have an inner part that isn't seen by outsiders. It's like a private joke that you keep hearing in your head, and it makes you giggle to yourself. Using recorded, stored sensory bits in the brain, you can relive instances vividly, be they positive or negative. It is like watching a movie: a mind-movie. The pictures of thoughts in your mind-movie transport you and create emotions as you view scenes. When you're sad you can try to lessen it by feeling the cheerful emotions of a happy mind-movie. A zipping, quick stimulus can snap an emotion on.

People with Autism are capable of forming pure, real attachments with others. Attachments can be scary, because the feelings accompanying them could swell too big. It's quite difficult to trust anybody, especially if you have been hurt badly by other people throughout your lifetime.

There are some things that can be done to try to avoid emotional fits. Here are some ideas:

1. Learn what things frighten the child and protect her from them. Also, never take away any of the objects the child is attached and devoted to.

2. When she gets alarmed, explain what is happening to her. Autistic people can reason. They can be highly intellectual. Therapists can assist with ways to keep the child calm.

3. Do not force affection on a child who is overwhelmed by it. Show affection in slow, tiny steps. Introduce soft, gentle caresses. Many children favour deep pressure and massage. Some, however, prefer only light petting.

4. If a tantrum or panic attack begins, it may help to distract the child's focus from her pain by touch. If she likes it, take her hand and tickle or rub the palm. Talk softly to her. Never reprimand. Never shout. On occasion the child will approach you and ask for comfort in her own way. Most times, the child won't do this, though, because it's quite difficult for autistics to ask for help.

5. Try to help the child grasp what will result in the immediate future. Autistics are confused about the concept of future. If they don't have it now, they can't foresee it. So, they also

think that unhappy events will go on forever. Try to find concrete ways to communicate to the child that she will feel better, the bad will pass. If the child can talk, type, or write, use words to explain. Keep explanations simple. The child is already confused. Drawing can help a lot, too. It doesn't matter how the drawing looks. It doesn't have to mean anything, either. Just get the child to do something other than focus on her anxiety. You can both communicate by drawing, just as with music. Play soothing music. Play music you know makes the child feel happy. Hop. Dance. Lie down on cushions. Sing. Hum.

6. If you are outside on a day of pleasant weather, try to get to an area where you can run or use swings. Exercise can reduce stress and release the inward energy of anger or fear.

7. Patience is always important. The child will sense when you get annoyed or frustrated, and will probably translate that into thinking you're angry directly with her.

8. Remember that emotions in Autism are basically not matched to the child's age in years. The brain may be advanced past age in years, but emotions are behind. An autistic adult or child probably will have the emotions of a much younger person. Barking 'Grow up!' isn't the answer. The emotional age of the person will always be younger than the person's years. There is nothing wrong with this. Society puts too much emphasis upon 'acting one's age'. People's behaviours shouldn't be measured on charts. The autistic person is autistic for life. Anything here that could apply to a child also can apply to an adult. Society seems afraid of grown-ups who cry or display strange emotions. That is too bad. Autistics are beyond social rules. They can be taught certain basic things, such as eating with utensils rather than with fingers. But, you cannot pick on an autistic person for every little thing. If an autistic man gets upset and cries in a supermarket, then something needs to be done to make him feel happier, not to ridicule him for his tears! If you get looks from other customers, tell them not to look.

People will always have something to complain about. Don't let them make you ashamed of your child. I do repeat: *don't let anyone make you ashamed of your autistic child!!* This is a terrible thing, both for you, and for the child who does not deserve shame placed upon him.

9. Try to keep home life consistent and pleasant. Many autistics don't do well being dragged on various errands. Try to create a daily safe routine without interruptions or chaos. Autistics cannot handle regular people's lives. They need limited upsets, a lot of love, and a feeling they are safe.

10. *Do not* ever tell an autistic you will do something, then not do it! An autistic expects you to do what you promised. It's not acceptable to use the big world way where language doesn't mean what its words say it means. If you can't do something, be honest and say so. An autistic person also doesn't understand excuses such as, 'I got too busy'.

11. The child's own emotions, and the emotions of others, can hurt. Most autistics are afraid of anger. Out-of-control feelings seem spooky and scary. They upset the whole body. This can be subtle or like a volcano. Define various emotions and explain them so the child can match her feelings with the words. It helps if she knows that the reason her whole body shakes and she cries is because she feels 'frustrated'. Emotions in an autistic can emerge in non-traditional ways. Understanding emotions is an abstract concept, and people with Autism do better with concrete concepts. However, once the child sort of learns to expect particular inside feelings connected to particular events, emotions won't seem as formidable. When they overwhelm, they become like an unknown, and they are unpredictable.

12. When taking the child to visit a doctor or dentist, explain what is going to happen; each child may need to visit several health care professionals until the one is found with whom the child feels most at ease. It's tricky to take an autistic person of any age to a new health care professional. The health care person should have an idea of what Autism is. It

is quite inexcusable for people working in the health field to be ignorant of Autism. They know what blindness, and Down Syndrome, and asthma are. They should also know Autism, since Autism affects all aspects of a person, and it is a delicate matter.

It's very upsetting for an autistic individual to go to any health practitioner. Examination requires touching in nearly every instance. It involves coming closer to the autistic person than her barriers allow. The doctor, nurse, dentist, or whomever must be extra understanding and patient, and must make no sudden moves or loud noises. The child's parent must be involved actively, as well, talking to the child, reassuring, and explaining. The health professional should tell the child everything before he does it. Do not say, 'This won't hurt' if you know damn well it will. It is far better to explain why an action will hurt and that it is actually going to make the sickness or injury or problem better. Do that even if you aren't sure the child is listening.

13. Emotions can be friends. It is human to be emotional. All creatures have many emotions. To be active in your child's life, yet to be aware of not running it, is going to help the well-being of the family. Try not to argue or fight in front of an autistic child. They are highly sensitive to this. A cloud of hostility in a household can leave terrible scars that harm an autistic person for life. Serious anger can crush the child. Things you might consider non-harmful actions such as certain punishments, could be devastating to the child. Also, some children react to traditional spankings in unique ways, such as by laughing, screaming, rejecting, abandoning, hitting, exposing the child to family quarrels, forcing the child into frightening situations, condemning the child, treating the child as less than others, embarrassing or shaming the child, threatening the child, blaming the child for ruining your life, all are abuse and are very wrong.

14. Never force touches or eye contact. It can be traumatic to the child, and cause a feeling of shock.

Rage is a major emotion in many autistic people's lives. They can grow up living with rage because they feel misunderstood, and that nobody was sympathetic to them. It's crucial to get an early diagnosis for your autistic little one. Do not be ashamed of going to a psychologist or a doctor (preferably a doctor) and explaining the child's behaviour. Early diagnosis is important because it helps the parent cope with, accept, and begin understanding the child early on. Ignoring or overlooking so-called eccentric or odd behaviour in the child leads only to ignorance and possible harm to the child in years ahead. Early diagnosis shouldn't be used as a start of trying to mold the autistic child into a non-autistic child. Diagnosis provides an answer to questions concerning the child's behaviour. It starts the family coming closer to each other, learning about each other. Many autistics never have that opportunity. That is tragic.

It's refreshing to see many present-day parents really loving their autistic children, and trying to understand them. Remember that autistic people are in need of their own lives. Nobody has any right to run their lives, or to make all of their decisions for them.

It's important to remember autistic children and grown-ups do love others. Emotions merely show themselves differently in Autism, and they may be more pronounced or less evident than another would expect. Nobody has a right to dictate how someone else should express himself or herself. I need to stress that the parent shouldn't feel his or her child doesn't care or doesn't love, or can't have fun, or can't play, or can't sometimes enjoy the company of others. Autistics will shy away from crowds, and can be very upset by strangers in the house. But they also can feel attached to one or two kind and patient friends. Autistics often are extremely delightful people, with innovative thoughts, who simply have their own way of living and observing things. They are generally very honest and make sane, realistic observations of what they experience. It is highly difficult to hide anything from them. They detect the emotions of other people. Often they reflect the emotions of others, so care must be taken to work on keeping the home atmosphere positive, loving, and balanced.

There are even autistics who get married, and may or may not bear children. This doesn't mean they've lost their Autism, or that they are only very mildly affected. It means they've found someone who finally understands, and who makes a fine friend and partner.

§

Communication and Language

Autism affects communication in a major way. Yet there must be communication in order to be understood, and to understand. It need not be in the form of speech; there are many forms of communication. The autistic child needs to be able to tell his needs and wants so he can feel in control and less dependent upon others.

Teaching programmes place too much emphasis on speech. Society expects every human being to speak, and looks down on those who won't or can't. A great number of people still consider a lack of speech to equate with a lack of brains. Language doesn't refer only to speech. Consider written language and sign language – even the wordless languages of animals and human body language.

Lack of spoken language isn't connected with a malfunction of the brain. An example of this is the author of this book, who does not speak. Another example is those non-verbal autistic children who are taught to use a communication device and begin writing profound poetry. There are various reasons for the cases of muteness in autistic people. Some have a motor inability to ever speak. Some speak well until they reach a certain age, then go silent. Some speak regularly with alternating periods of selective mutism. And some have no type of mutism at all.

Selective mutism is when the person chooses whom to talk to, and in which situations. Many times the person talks to family in the home, but won't talk in public, or in unfamiliar surroundings. The stress of strangers being present and a new environment greatly affect how and if the person speaks.

Elective mutism is electing to be silent to everyone. Autistics can have periods of either type which last a lifetime, or several years or weeks. It is quite difficult for the autistic who is selectively mute to find sympathy because outsiders say, 'Well, why can't you speak all the time, then?'

For someone who takes the ease of speaking for granted, it's impossible to explain why. But the autistic person doesn't always plan when he will or won't speak. He isn't trying to be rude by not speaking to another person, nor is he showing dislike of that person.

In many cases of mutism the child feels too overwhelmed to speak. Speaking involves emotion, and is highly complex. Some autistics fall mute when they feel confused. Sometimes there is a fear of speaking. Talking is a gift, but it is also a choice. Someone who doesn't feel comfortable speaking shouldn't be made to talk. There are deaf people who either can't or won't speak. It's no earth-smashing horror to not talk.

A non-talking person can use other means of communicating. This should definitely be done, since the autistic person is always in danger of becoming a victim. Some people try to take advantage of them. Many people try to tell others what it is that an autistic individual wants or likes or needs. They guess without knowing. They can be ignorant of the autistic's struggles to communicate. In that case, more care must be taken to learn how to interpret autistic languages. It's easier for the non-autistic to put himself in the autistic's place than the other way round.

It is neat to be very different. But it hurts to be constantly misunderstood. It's scary to feel abandoned, totally alone, and unaided. In Autism there is isolation. It's not a bad thing. A withdrawn personality isn't a terrible thing that needs to be changed. Some people like being withdrawn and rather isolated. Some autistic people prefer being alone and rather secluded. These individuals may never have a social life the same as others. There's nothing wrong with living a quiet, shy life and remaining sheltered, as long as the person is happy.

The mere fact that an autistic child or adult uses speech doesn't mean his Autism is not severe. Severity is determined by how thoroughly Autism affects a person overall. It does not mean that the more severely autistic person is always mentally retarded, or in all cases completely unable to communicate or to take care of himself. There are indeed people who are considered to be, and formally diagnosed as fairly severely autistic, and who also can cook, drive a car limited distances, can communicate well using some form of language, and are even snappy dressers and voracious readers. The author of this text is one of them.

All individuals with Autism do have some communication difficulties. Communication is tied directly to relating to others, and autistic people relate in very non-traditional ways. What is usually lacking in some way is expressive speech. As mentioned before, speaking is connected with emotion. Someone who has very confusing, large emotions can find it extremely hard to speak in certain situations. Sensory experiences can really affect the act of talking. Many autistic children and grown-ups find the ring of human voices unpleasant. This can include their own voice. Speaking can be such an overwhelming task, much too stimulating, too tiring, too frightening, even, to do. Something like that can be emotionally painful.

And it can be most harrowing if it is an act others expect every human being to do effortlessly, every day, without thinking of the stress or inability of the special-needs person. Something so simple as speaking is not second nature to one who has serious difficulty with it. In that case, it can feel amazingly foreign. The non-verbal or selectively-mute autistic individual can feel as if he's going to explode, or unravel and scatter away into the wind if he is forced to utter one word under duress. He will lose his feeling of centredness. He will feel as though parts of him are breaking loose and floating – as if he is losing himself just by projecting his voice outward into the space beyond his body. He would be traumatized by talking.

Understanding the complexities of language and how it is formed in non-autistic people is something that hasn't yet been accomplished. Many people consider there to be an 'abnormality' in autistic communication. Call it whatever you will. I am against using the words 'abnormal' and 'normal.' Abnormal is derogatory. I feel the same about using the term, 'a failure'. Autism doesn't imply failure. It doesn't imply that the autistic person is only an incomplete human. This is what some professionals still seem to think.

Communication in Autism is not a 'failure'. It is not non-existent. It's simply different, in some way eccentric in an interesting way, and in some cases dormant. When a totally non-verbal child learns to use a communication device, it's liberating – not liberation from Autism, but liberation from being unable to tell any one of her loves, desires, feelings. Many texts speak of communication as a release from the prison of Autism. Autism is not a prison. And there are other conditions that can result in mutism caused by various physical changes. Individuals who have suffered stroke are the example that pops first into my head. This is vastly different from autistic types of mutism. People who are silenced by stroke have most likely spoken all of their lives. They aren't autistic and so they've learned speech the regular way at the regular age. In Autism, the fundamental workings of learning to talk are distorted. Speech has a purpose. Some children with Autism are unsure of its purpose. The main purpose of speech is to communicate. Autistics often use the speech they have in ways other than communication with another individual. They talk to themselves more than to others. They also often enjoy repeating specific phrases and words. They pick certain words or tunes that they favour. The ring of these in their minds feels nice as a form of self-stimulation. So, there definitely is a purpose for them doing this. It is not meaningless. It probably is meaningless to a non-autistic. But that doesn't mean to say that it should be eliminated. Other basically non-communicative uses of speech in Autism include choosing a word, phrase, or tune, and repeating it to yourself when you feel stressed. It is a way of calming yourself.

As mentioned in the previous chapter, senses play an enormous part in this. Imagine that you simply love the sound of the words 'purple fur'. Don't consider what the words' actual definitions are. Only pretend you feel vocal intonation. Pretend it makes you shiver in glee, as well as feeling relaxed. This is a lot like using mantras in meditation. Whenever you become upset, you turn to your own little mantra to help you focus inside yourself, and comfort yourself. You can use your special private words to just feel good, too. Repeated in sequence, it makes calmness settle over you, 'Purple fur, purple fur, purple fur'. Also, words can sound funny and make you giggle.

Echolalia is a common characteristic of Autism. Repeating things other people say helps to clarify the meaning in an autistic person's mind. It aids cognitive processes. An autistic will repeat a question someone asks her to be able to hear the words in her own voice – to take an external stimulus inward, accept it and prepare a reply. Some autistic people don't mind answering questions. Some get freaked out by it. But to ask a question is initiating a conversation. Many autistics can't hold traditional conversation. Most are puzzled by the rules of conversation; it's the two-way exchange and the pauses and taking and giving that confuse them. It's something outside of themselves (the other person) interacting with what is inside them.

It sometimes is deeply annoying to have another person trying to communicate with an autistic. The autistic reels threatened. A small action from another can be interpreted as a threat so it is important to try to help the autistic parson realise that no harm is intended.

Although the complex usage of language is spread over the entire brain, it is the left hemisphere that is mainly responsible for its formation. The left hemisphere concerns itself mostly with language and analytical skills, whilst the right hemisphere concerns itself mainly with musical memory, spatial skills and creative thinking. Therefore, it is said that right-handed people are governed by the left sides of their brain, since whatever hemisphere is dominant governs the opposite side of the body. There are exceptions to this. In Autism it seems that many times, the child switches hand-dominance. Neither one nor the other is favoured constantly. I began babyhood preferring to use my left hand. Then, I picked up some right-handed tasks. I am now ambidextrous, which means I use one hand for certain tasks and the other for different ones. I prefer to hold my pen in my right hand. I eat with either left or right hand. I do a lot of reaching and cleaning with my left hand. It seems that in Autism, impulses aren't governed strictly by one portion of the brain, as in non-autistic people. Autism is more a right-brained condition, no matter which hand the person prefers. Studies have compared some autistic traits to the traits or people who have lesions on their left hemispheres. Lesions can result in loss of speech or loss of the knowledge of what speech is for, as well as special types of aphasias and apraxias.

As there is a right to speak, there is a right to be silent. Some nuns and monks in various religions take vows of silence. Silence is contemplative. It connects you to your deepest self. Autism is a unique form of isolated personality, not a medical tragedy. It makes sense that there often is mutism in Autism.

Yet it is the right of all beings to communicate. So, if a person either cannot speak, or finds it overwhelmingly painful for whatever reason, there are other options: facilitated communication, picture boards that have words identifying the objects pictured above them, typing, writing, sign language. Even extremely simple words can be tacked together to form a type of language an autistic child can use. The parent must be patient and intuitive. Learning language is fun. The autistic child will feel more independent to be able to ask for a glass of juice with words, signed, spoken, or written.

Communication will help the autistic person gain more control of her world. As the child begins to learn the meanings of emotions, nouns, verbs, and is newly able to understand words and perhaps read, the vast chaos of the outside becomes less scary. This is wonderful. The aim is to help the child feel more comfortable. When the fear lessens, then the child is more free … not less autistic, but more at ease and happy.

Studying the scientific causes of the brain structural differences that make communication and language oddities in Autism is necessary. But it doesn't tell how an autistic person feels inside as she goes through experiences. The studies must be done out of concern and deep interest in a unique type of person, rather than trying to discover a way to eradicate this type of person.

Often autistic communication is speckled with charming individual idiosyncrasies, such as colourful adjectives and original phrases. That is quite useful when writing poetry. Art can be used as a mode of communication, too. Opening the eyes to look deep, to feel with the bottom of your heart, to love freely is the way to live with an autistic one. Although they may not be able always to tell someone, they need an enormous amount of love. When they acquire a way of communicating it also helps parents and other loved ones get to know the autistic person. The specific child or adult now has the means to translate her large emotions into spoken or silent words. A beautiful spirit is discovered. This fragile spirit can now tell another, 'Purple is my favourite colour', or 'I love jazz", or 'I'm not hungry any more', or 'I want a hug'.

Some autistic people never achieve a level of language usage on the level of a complex conversation. It is a lot easier for them to use language for technical or concrete purposes than to try to describe emotions. I doubt there is an autistic alive who doesn't have some type of emotional and communication eccentricities. In a way, they explain the reason for some of the social withdrawal and discomfort that is another main trait of this condition. Some autistics want to start a conversation but have no idea how. There is a desire to be left alone, because they naturally have an inward personality. Yet, sometimes an interest in other people contradicts that autistic aloneness. Without the confidence or knowledge to approach and engage other people, there is a feeling of alienation. Some autistics are happier spending much of their time by themselves, or perhaps with music as their only companion. Even when they are engulfed by other people, the stand out with their unique, apparent lack of interest. They often seem unaware of others. They appear as unusual, mysterious Martians who don't know the culture of the planet they have been misplaced upon. In a home busting with interacting children, the autistic child will hover on the outskirts, disconnected, floating along his own path. This is what is meant by autistic aloneness. It doesn't have to mean lonely. It's more of a term to describe the social, language, and developmental characteristics of Autism combined. Each one of these influences the others. Some individuals who have Autism are timid and shy; others will easily approach people. All have a distinct form of inner aloneness.

Human language involves indirectness. It is the subtleties that are baffling to an autistic. They have difficulty grasping the same word or meaning in different contexts. It is sometimes hard for the youngster to understand that words which sound the same can be spelled another way, thereby meaning something completely different. When they learn one word they just don't know that it can have variables. The brain is fragmented, not as easily functioning together as a smooth whole. Being able to read greatly helps the autistic with mastering language. Some autistic children who are very bright actually teach themselves how to read at an early age, but they may not show outsiders that they can read. Talents and gifts of the autistic person often are discovered by accident. It is highly difficult to explain to an autistic that the word 'die' is not the same as the word 'dye'. They hear that both have an identical sound, so they are influenced by that first.

Autistic children who read early often get an extensive vocabulary and become excellent spellers. The left hemisphere of their brains is apparently fairly highly developed. However they will still have certain limitations in other types of communication, and they will be socially inept. Or they also may be able to use correctly unusual, difficult words, but not know that a baby cat is called a kitten. In Autism, a lot of the assimilation from others in learning isn't present. The children don't automatically pick everything up from parents and teachers. In educating an autistic child in language and communication, it's important to stay aware of this fact. Don't take it for granted that the child will already know what others know. Autistics have a flair for remembering facts and storing knowledge in their brains, computer-style. But they don't usually pick up nuances or common knowledge facts. Something that is not actually learned from a voice or a book is much harder for an autistic to grasp. Rather than fight this fact, go with it. Take it into consideration that some people will be more innocent and naive than others.

KRISHNA & RADHA

Even non-verbal autistics who can't type, or write, or sign, have a form of inner language. All autistics have their own understanding of language that is private to them. Non-autistics need to allow for individual creativity in communication. Not everything has to be as rigid and forbidding as a grammar textbook. If the autistic is too restricted, he probably will stop communicating altogether. You can't dictate what mode of communication your child must use. You must find the one that is most naturally suited to him. It is certainly not true that Autism is characterized by failure to communicate, or inability, or not enough intelligence. It is more accurate to say that they can communicate, and their style is rather distinct, and each is different. All living creatures are born with some type of communication. This shouldn't ever be stifled. The autistic person needs freedom. You can't box someone into a square by demanding she communicate exactly how you dictate and expect.

A non-verbal autistic shouldn't have to rely solely upon others for communication. She should have a special communication device as well as a talking phone. It's not fair for her to be made to wait on somebody else to do a task. She needs to do things for herself, even if someone is taking care of her in other ways. So the prime purpose of helping an autistic person communicate is to help her feel good about herself and to enjoy the rights that others have.

One final tip: remember that a non-verbal autistic that types or writes does have a voice; it's just communicating. Some autistics need to type slowly. Their co-ordination isn't developed enough, yet their brains are whizzing, so it becomes frustrating. You must allow them to express fully what it is they try to say. Do not interrupt, or interject what you think they might be trying so painstakingly to tell you. That is their way of talking. They deserve the same courtesy as people who speak get when they're engaged in a conversation.

§

Intelligence, Autism, and Savant Skills

Frequently, autistic people's intelligence is underestimated. Many professionals still claim that the majority of autistics score within the mentally retarded range on IQ tests. This doesn't mean the majority of them are mentally retarded, however. There's a lot more to overall intelligence then an IQ test can show. There are also different types of retarded. The word retarded doesn't mean stupid. It means slow in development. As Autism is a developmental condition, all autistic people are retarded in some aspect. They are behind peers of their same age in some way. This doesn't necessarily mean they are not as intelligent as their peers. A person can be retarded socially, retarded mentally, retarded emotionally, retarded developmentally. To be retarded in some way isn't a terrible thing to be ashamed of.

I refuse to use the terms 'low-functioning' and 'high-functioning' when referring to Autism. These are misleading terms. They are defined by the big world as being more able to do a task, or less able. But the tasks unfailingly are tasks that non-autistic people do. Big world people can be considered idiots in the autistic world, too, just as it can be the other way round. Idiot certainly is a derogatory term. Yet it's still used by taunting humans and some members of the medical realm when mentioning what was called years ago the 'idiot savant' (mostly autistic people who displayed very superior skills in fragmented areas).

At first, the public considered autistics to be what now is called low-functioning. It meant that nearly all were thought to be mentally retarded, unfeeling, mute, with no self-help skills and an extremely remote personality. The general public is still very ill-informed about

Autism. It basically holds the view that if an autistic person drives a car or rides a horse very well, that person can't possibly be truly autistic. That view is totally incorrect. Even if an individual does test in the range of mental retardation, there can be several reasons:

1. Obviously, that person may actually be mentally retarded.

2. The person didn't completely grasp how to respond to the testing questions.

3. The person may be annoyed by the questions and simply refuse to answer them, or purposely answer questions incorrectly. This frequently happens with a highly intelligent child who is bored and frustrated.

4. The individual's personal Autism may largely prevent the correct answers from being given. A 'short circuit' may be occurring in the brain. The correct answer awaits within the brain – but it gets lodged and can't be transfered outwards to lips or to paper. It is a freezing up that is very often caused by stress.

Society places too much emphasis upon mere IQ test results. Try to go beyond that. See the evidences of intelligence as a whole. The non-autistic world must be able to gather all information into a whole when dealing with a human being. A human being deserves to be treated better than as a number or as a machine. Don't just see one aspect of a person and label the entire person with one word. People can get quite snobby about their college degrees, or their cars, or their memberships in MENSA. It's almost as if some people introduce themselves by announcing, 'Hi, I'm a genius, and I'm a member of MENSA'. Of course, very high intelligence is a marvellous thing, and the author of this book is far from stupid. Learning and intelligence grow for our entire lives. They are vital and real. But intelligence should not be a limiting word. It encompasses so much.

I believe there are intelligences that can't be measured. I believe Autism is one of these. Autistic people must be discovered. They must be coached to reach their potential. They are worth much more than being subjected to idiotic therapies, which push them to repeat endless tiny tasks. Use tiny tasks as stepping-stones to mysteries beyond.

Autistic people must be allowed to live their lives the way they please. They need to feel happy about themselves and be proud of who they are.

Their gifts are formidable assets. Even autistics who aren't savants have special gifts, which aren't present in non-autistics. Autistic people naturally are better at simply being themselves. They are not magicians. They should never be criticized or called stupid because of the way they live. People who are adept at focusing attention like a laser beam are people who can retain details. The tiniest details they notice escape other people's attention. Minute details are important, too. They exist. Plus, they can build upon one another to create big details.

Savant gifts are present from birth. They are honed, as the person grows older. A misconception is that only mentally slow autistics can be savants. I am a savant in music, writing poetry, drawing, and some electronics. Savants are amazing, fascinating people. They may never be able to live completely independently. Some of them never grasp the complexities of regular human life enough to be able to drive a car, or to look after a bank account by themselves. Yet they have one or more very superior gifts which they can perform better than other people can. Also, there are those savants who do very well at many things; they have their specific savant abilities, combined with a knack for picking things up rapidly (one sign of the type of intelligence measurable on IQ tests), and they are whizzes at various things. They thirst for knowledge. They are insatiable.

Contrary to what a few teachers still believe, most autistics enjoy learning. There are many examples of this. If an autistic is interested in learning, but is unable to get others to teach her, she will find a way to teach herself. Sometimes communication skills aren't developed enough to tell others what she wants to learn about. Other times, too many surrounding people don't have faith in this 'autistic cripple'. That's a dangerous attitude: As pointed out in an earlier chapter, autistics can sense other people's emotions. If other people are condescending, and have no faith in the special child or adult, he will begin picking that up and have no faith in himself.

Autism can present itself as a learning disability. But Autism does not mean that different techniques must be used. There must be much more individualized attention. There must be a quiet environment so as not to distract or startle the child. Autistic youngsters usually fear other children.

Frequently they will hide their skills, surprising others later on. Being self-taught is one sign of high intelligence. Savants are not taught their skills. They do enjoy them, or they wouldn't use them. Books have been written on this subject alone. Doctors study what goes on in the savant brain. It is a paradox that one with Autism, the most severe and debilitating type of development disability, can also be gifted with examples of genius in music, mathematics, visual art, computers, and so on. Some people's argument is that a true genius is gifted in almost everything. As stated before, there are some savant autistics who do many things very well, besides their splinter skills. Also, consider the examples of Thomas Edison and Wolfgang Amadeus Mozart. Thomas Edison was considered a dunce in school, and he performed poorly on tests and in various subjects. Then he discovered what he excelled in: inventing, and mechanical engineering. Mozart was brilliant in music, but could not manage money. He also was considered very odd in social situations. Both of these men, by the way, as well as many other brilliant men and women of science and the arts, exhibit autistic traits. These two are not considered fully autistic, however.

There seems to be a connection between genius and Autism. Often the siblings of autistic children are non-autistic and very bright. Autism can occur in any nation, any culture, and any income bracket. Yet a lot of it is genetic. Parents may show some traits, such as obsessiveness, resistance to changes, amazing attention to detail, preference of being by themselves. Then it is passed on to the child, who inherits a few things from either parent, then is born with many of his own traits. So the child ends up being truly autistic.

Intelligence is also hereditary. To me, this connection between brilliance and Autism isn't a coincidence. Autism is most likely a very unique special type of genius. The studies that deal with this intelligence should be aimed at appreciating the distinctly autistic mind, rather than pointing out what freaks people think autistics are.

Autistics are picture thinkers. They see their thoughts. Things happen like a movie in their minds, to provide concrete basis for understanding what is going on around them. Vivid images make things come alive. Autistics are always thinking, thinking, thinking. They are often described as being far from intellectual. But actually, being immersed in their inner kingdoms, their minds are constantly actively doing many things: trying to synchronize their built-in rhythms, striving to keep themselves feeling safe, dissecting the meanings of endless stimuli, soaking up interesting information, reliving pleasurable events. It's difficult for them to settle down mentally. Relaxation and stress-lessening techniques can benefit them. But they should retain their edge because it fuels them. Their mind-movies and the other things happening in their brains can tend to get jumbled. So outside things easily distract them in a learning environment, especially if they become bored or upset.

Learning should take advantage of the autistic tendency to perseverate on one topic. It actually feels neat to become obsessed with something I like. I plunge into it, let it surround me, I become its essence. Many times the obsessions go from one to the next as an autistic person gets older. In this way, the person learns and retains information and emotional experiences dealing with various topics. Obsessions are connected with emotions. Some people have unhappy obsessions; some have obsessions that are mostly exciting. Of course if you have an obsessive nature – and autistics do have – you're going to automatically obsess about nearly everything. Autistics are so highly sensitive that they experience everything like a lightning bolt. A thing that acts as a small annoyance, a buzzing fly, to a regular person, will seem like a massive irritation or even fear, a giant gnawing mosquito, to them. Obsessing about fun and stimulating things helps to stabilize crazy emotions. Obsessions may tire someone else, or may seem strange. But obsessions are part of life for those who live in Autism.

Obsessions also can be combined with savant skills. If a person has a remarkable memory for music and reproducing it on a piano, then that can be used as a topic for education. Savant abilities shouldn't be discouraged or altered. They come from the person naturally and must be allowed to come about freely. If an autistic child is a piano prodigy and reproduces compositions he heard on the radio, it might do more harm than good to try to push music theory on him. By trying to force him to read music, you're not going to make him into a concert pianist. You may confuse him and make him unhappy. Savant skills must flow. It often seems as if he is a stream gushing forth from a very tiny crack. Savant skills involve memory and superior sense organs, and an uncanny fixating ability.

When Leo Kanner formally gave the condition known as Autism its name, he described his first bunch of autistic children as having potential for high intelligence. He was astute enough to recognize non-traditional signs of unusual gifts. It was only later that people began to speak of autistics as mentally slow. Why do so many people still think that all autistic people are mentally retarded? The fact is, if one is completely truly mentally retarded, one cannot do what an autistic person can do.

As mentioned earlier, being non-verbal is not an indication of low intelligence. It's more a brain that is different, and naturally is more inclined to think in pictures than in words. This resembles the brain of a person born deaf, who never heard speech and can't think in words. A deaf child can't hear the sounds of words in his head, so it is hard for him to learn to speak. Yet he has gifts and a sensitivity, another way of experiencing things that a hearing child doesn't have.

Autism is more like being deaf or blind combined with other phenomena than it is like being brain-dysfunctional. I don't consider something to be wrong with those who are born deaf or blind. I consider them simply to not be able to hear or see. So, in Autism, there is a variance in how the brain processes information, how it functions, and how the person develops. This variance doesn't mean there is something terribly wrong which needs to be fixed. Just because something doesn't do what other things do doesn't make it broken. This can be viewed from the other side, as well, since regular people can't do what autistic savants can do. This issue is about humans, not machines.

Most autistics have superb memories for details. They can memorize minutely dissected information. Some savants memorize entire routes of underground trains. Some snap mental photographs of objects, then draw them perfectly later on. Some record musical pieces in their minds, then hum or play them flawlessly on an instrument later on. Some savants can count extremely rapidly, and have an aptitude for mathematics. Many have gifts in figuring out electronics and computers. Some savants have a combination of these or other gifts. These visual thinkers have an ability to construct a completed picture in their minds, and then draw it, or use it for references. That is why those autistics that have a gift for grammar can spell so excellently. As they read, they quickly memorize the spellings of words. Often their reading levels far exceed their ages. When they misspell a word they can refer to their mental catalogue of data to recall which spelling looks more accurate. These abilities aren't learned at school. They come innately as the autistic teaches herself – most likely in private. Savant skills have been examined, but no one has proven exactly how they work. They are influenced by the autistic 'desire for the preservation of sameness' in their environments. Autistics need order and precision to feel safe. They strive to control their immediate small worlds. They create an elaborate personal, tightly controlled network to do this: to keep themselves comfortably shielded and cocooned in their own bubbles. This feat definitely requires a complicated, intelligent mind.

Some people of the vast outside world complain, saying some savant gifts are useless – such as a two-year-old memorizing where all the stop signs appear on a specific travelling route. No gift is useless, however. No intelligence is in vain. Even if a certain gift or learned talent can never be used as a career, it is still not purposeless. It exists as a part of an individual. One displayed gift is evident of others that may be dormant. Some savants prefer to keep various gifts to themselves. It's important never to push an autistic person to achieve something somebody else wants for her. She can't live the life of someone else. She needs to live her own life – even if it's a quietly shy life; even if it's a life that others think is wacky.

So, behind the so-called 'empty stare' of an autistic person is an entire wee universe. Parents discover that their child is actually more aware of what is happening around her than she appears to be. The child sits isolated, seemingly ignoring everything. But she is watching from the sides of her eyes. Her ears pick up all conversation. She is probably curious, but not showing it. She notices whenever anything is moved in the house. She notices any new clothes because her senses are well informed. She may correct something somebody said when nobody even thinks she was paying attention.

It is quite painful to be considered an incompetent idiot because you're autistic. Do keep in mind how that can hurt, and also what a lie it can be. Learning about different individuals with Autism will open eyes to interesting and delightful discoveries. It is a way to travel new pathways to other minds.

§

Discrimination

Autism in itself isn't a hell. The hell comes from a society that refuses to accept people or try to accommodate them. They are still pushed away so people can try to forget they exist. Discrimination can come from the public, the home, the schools, the physicians and the government. All of them combine to form an image of a cruel, united enemy which wants only that the autistic stop being autistic and join the 'real world'.

It doesn't work like that. First, Autism is incurable. Second, the autistic's private world is as real as the outside world of everybody.

An autistic child's bliss can end when he begins school. Some autistic children attend regular school; some go to special school. I think they should go to a unique school with a lot of teacher attention. Mainstreaming is a bad idea in many cases. Non-autistic classmates aren't prepared to deal with the autistic youngster. Putting one special child in with a mass of regular children is cause for disaster. School can be a completely disruptive tragedy for the highly sensitive, eccentric autistic child. His behaviour brings attention to him. But rather than punish or reprimand the other children when they torment him, teachers punish the autistic himself and try to force him to change to fit in.

Children should not be taught that to blend in is always best. If someone is different, that is not a crime. It's something to be proud of. Autistic people should be proud of themselves. Negative messages bombard them from all angles. Many times they can't find peace even at home, for the torment continues there.

Imagine what it is like to be laughed at simply because you are very different from others. Nothing you do is good enough for them.

Nothing about you pleases them. They don't want to be your friend. The autistic child is pictured ever alone, described as having no friends. Part of this is due to their own natures being introverted and being baffled by the actions of other people. Part of this is because very few people want to have an autistic friend. People make that very clear. They call the autistic boy or girl an assortment of cruel names: 'Retard', 'Idiot', 'Freak', 'Weirdo', and other taunts tailored to the individual. Children do not merely tease. They taunt, torture, torment, ostracize, alienate and even sometimes hit, spit on, and throw objects at someone they decide not to like for whatever petty, asinine reason. Usually they get away with it because the teacher does nothing to protect the child being hurt.

Imagine simply being yourself, and that your self is naturally different. You have no idea why all of your classmates hate you. Imagine living through this abuse every day of the school season. Imagine growing up with this abuse. Imagine your classmates bullying you, trying to physically harm you by hurling large balls at you in the playground. Imagine it is your very first day of school. You are very sensitive and are already overwhelmed by blaring fluorescent lighting and unknown voices echoing eerily off the walls. You don't fully understand why you are in this frightening new building, because you have difficulties with communication. You have fierce attachments to your mother, who has been you main companion for the early years of your small life. (Contrary to what many books report, children with Autism can effectively form strong attachments to a parent.)

But, now your mother is pulling at your tiny hand, leading you towards a teacher who looms large and strange. All of your senses are overwhelmed. Then your beloved companion who has kept you safe up until now starts to leave you. Autistic children sometimes aren't distressed when a parent leaves them. Sometimes they are, however, and that varies with each individual. There can be a symbolic attachment to a trusted parent, a fear of being abandoned into the jaws of the big world.

Imagine you are falling to bits, feeling confused, shattered, so you start to rock your body to comfort yourself with rhythm of your world. You are fragile. You will be fragile for as long as you live, although you can learn to be a strong fighter, and indeed you must do so if you are to remain intact and let nobody destroy you.

Now imagine your mother has left you in the classroom with completely unknown people. Many autistic little ones throw a wild tantrum at this point. It is not because they are naughty. It is because they are afraid. Even if they are verbal, it's so hard to explain this concept of school to them because it involves all new events. It is unpredictable.

Imagine the other children sensing in you something different immediately. They aren't drawn to it. They are repelled by it. They whisper to one another. They laugh at your rocking and say you are crazy. You shrink away, enfolding inside yourself, the walls of your mighty, autistic fortress, thick and tall. Inside this fortress your battle begins. It is this blessed silent strength within you that fortifies you throughout your life. It is all you have. Nobody else truly ever understands, unless he or she also has an autistic mind.

Everybody may suffer being made fun of at some point. But it's nothing compared to the endless, vicious torment endured daily by those unfortunate-fortunate individuals who stand out because of a major difference. I call them unfortunate because their difference sentences them to cruel treatment. I call them fortunate because they are truly blessed by being unique, and if they don't give in to others, their pain will make them stronger. They will have gone through various types of abuse and will have emerged triumphant. Triumph comes from remaining true to oneself. Triumph comes from knowing who you are and never allowing outsiders to change you. Sometimes autistic children are confused by the concept of self versus non-self – what is 'me', and what is 'not me'. But they are humans who are fully developed, just developed into someone unusual. They are not incomplete. Often the part that is the 'not me' is muddled into what is 'me'. Autistic people are often oppressed by others. Their true personalities, which are noticeably autistic, are repressed because they irritate or disturb or annoy or confound others. So the autistic person mimics others to try to fit in, just so the awful pain of being made fun of stops. As an autistic person grows older, her real personality can get buried beneath the ones that are more socially acceptable. That is harmful and forms scars. Every creature is born with the right to be happy and to be who she or he is meant to be. By forcing an autistic person to act like everybody else, that basic right is stripped away.

People of the vast outside world of non-Autism must try to put themselves in the place of the autistic. They need to obtain an accurate description of what it feels like to be a person who is constantly picked on, reprimanded, or trained to act like somebody else. Autistic people do not fit into the molds of society. This fact is no excuse for the poor treatment so very many of them receive. Thankfully, a lot of them do have loving parents. The parent who is interested in easing the child's school pain should be sure to provide a stable, peaceful home full of love. A team of caring people may be needed: family members, a friendly, open-minded, knowledgeable doctor, and a well-trained private therapist. Since it is a law and a basic right for everyone to receive an education, the autistic child must find a way to cope with the learning process. In almost all cases, this way probably would be to avoid going to a regular mainstreamed school. Finding a relaxed atmosphere where the child can learn at her own pace, and where her condition will be appreciated, and where she will get the attention she needs is the best option. Also, she must be free from all taunting of other people. Autistic children are excruciatingly sensitive almost always. They find it impossible to ignore it when someone is making fun of them. They do take it deeply personally. Some non-autistic children are by nature more sensitive than others, of course. An autistic child is probably more sensitive than even the most sensitive of those.

Here is where the teacher can step in. The taunting of special youngsters must be stopped. The teacher must never allow taunts to go unnoticed. Children who do not understand about their autistic classmate must be taught. There are many children who giggle or sneer at other kids only because they are afraid of their differences, or because their friends do it, or because they do not understand. Once they become comfortable with the child who is unique, they can swiftly grow to like her. Then there are some children who can't tolerate any kind of deviation from anyone's norm. Perhaps they are taught to hate and fear someone who is different from themselves by their parents. I doubt that children are naturally so discriminatory. Actually, it doesn't matter what the reason is for seriously hurting somebody who has done nothing to you. It is wrong to hurt someone. An autistic child often can't stand up for himself. When surrounded by a bunch of taunting classmates, the child becomes overwhelmed. There are instances where a young autistic person will lash out in frustrated rage and strike or bite someone else. Not all autistic children are timid. But when something happens to cause the child to retaliate or even to initiate a miniature battle, it must be remembered that there is a reason for the behaviour. The teacher needs to supervise the autistic student as well as protect and be a friend who is an astute observer. School shouldn't be a place of pain. Many unusual young people end up detesting school and feeling afraid and anxious. Home schooling is a rather promising option for the autistic child who just can't get into a satisfactory situation at a school building. The child's happiness and well being are what is most important. If she cannot have happiness whilst she is learning, then the purpose of learning is defeated.

Discrimination from society weighs heavily on people with handicaps for their lifetimes. There are autistic adults who don't have jobs. This doesn't make them useless. It shouldn't make their families ashamed of them. They can't help having Autism. In many instances the stress of regular big world lives, and the restrictions of jobs and dealing with people are too much for the autistic individual to handle. Yet if he applies for disability living allowance for assistance from the government, he is then discriminated against by the government for being disabled. The government drags him through months of idiotic treatment. It makes promises it doesn't uphold. It tries to strip him of the dignity every human has. He also should not be put into an institution then forgotten there. That practice is actually fading out in the present era, fortunately. Autistic people have been released from large institutions into smaller environments better suited to them, such as private group homes and supervised apartments.

Some people with rather severe Autism are brilliant and able to do many personal things for themselves, yet cannot hold a job. They desire happy lives of their own, yet need assistance. It is no sin to need help or ask for it. Autistic people need shields against the chaotic outside world. They need guidance without having their daily lives dictated by others. The type of help they do not need is being nagged and discriminated against.

Imagine yourself a special disabled child. You're picked on by your teacher. You're attacked by your classmates who say things to you such as, 'Go away. We don't want you here with us. You're really weird,' or even, 'We hate you'. And don't think this sort of thing doesn't happen. It can happen in any school. It was done to me. I lived with it for years. Perhaps it requires a great deal of imagination for you to imagine what it's like to walk into a frightening, bright, noisy classroom on your very first day of school and be shunned by the other children. Listen to them sneer at you, 'We don't like you. We don't want you to sit at our table.' Feel how that stings. You're very shy so you can't tell anyone else about it. Your parents never find out most of what happens to you. Soon it all becomes a pathetic game. You put on a show for the little beasts that make fun of you; they're going to laugh at you no matter what you do, anyway. But then if they find out you can do something marvellous, such as play the piano or draw pictures, they suddenly want to be your friends. A lot of them never change. They grow up like that, and their two-faced, fickle behaviour only continues in another form.

Children must be educated about Autism. There are programmes beginning in the schools that expose mainstreamed children to children with disabilities. When they get exposed to all different types of people they won't be as shocked and repelled by the presence of an autistic classmate. No child deserves to be put through daily torment, whether disabled or regular. The general public internationally is still largely ignorant of Autism. It is even worse in underdeveloped nations. Yet autistic people live in every nation and come into all cultures. So they can't simply be hidden away and ignored. That practice would be denying their existence and removing their rights.

Discrimination is hideous, whether it be directed towards whites, Asians, blacks, mentally retarded, blind, mute, deaf, Jews, American Indians, overweight people, thin people, women, children, men, lesbians, gays, or autistics. There are far too many people in so-called civilized societies who hate anyone who doesn't do things exactly as they do. People are hated for ludicrous reasons, even such as being quite shy and gentle rather than a violent gang member. So much of Autism is described as being terrible and negative. That description isn't the true Autism. Many people with this condition are abused, or are treated as though they are criminals. Some families are ashamed of them. The family members seem to be the ones who are pitied by the public: 'You must have tremendous strength to be able to cope with such a child.'

Autistic children are not a pox. They are not put upon this earth to bring their families pain. Before condemning an autistic child, take time to ponder the things you consider negative about him. Contrast that to what can be negative in other individuals. Consider a violent society with rapists, murderers, and people who shoot others with semi-automatic rifles. Put it all into a perspective. Try to see the precious gift that your own child is. Through your special and different little one, you can learn new things, and you can experience love in a fresh glow.

Do try to remember that the vast big world is still an unhappy place for your sensitive child. Yet autistic people can be joyful. They can be happy. You as the caretaker or parent must actively help. A home must be a safe haven. The unique person must be able to feel loved and wanted. He must feel cherished and protected. When so many cruel incidents can occur to the individual with Autism, she must be comforted in the home. The home is the very best place for education and for happy safety. Home can be moved from one town to another, from one nation to another. But it must remain constant in its core of love and acceptance. It must never, ever be a place of resentment, fear, or discrimination.

Techniques to 'assist' autistic young adults often fall quite short of their aims. Some of the organizations that claim to want to provide services to autistics really don't do a good job of it. Other programmes still insist upon changing the individual to become more acceptable to the masses. Consider spending most of your life in some sort of training which tries to remold you into fitting the expectations and wants of others. Unfortunately, many autistics are stuck in a dead end where nobody believes in them. They begin their education in a special school then stay in school long into adulthood. The adults often attend day centres where they have therapists who continue to work on their behaviour, speech, and social relations. Autism affects all aspects of a person, so an individual who has the condition can be therapied to death! It's unfair to expect somebody to spend a lifetime in training to be someone else. Intelligent, caring therapists can help the autistic one to achieve her potential. But she must still be allowed to remain autistic.

There are so many therapies for autistics that they become muddled. Rather than choose six separate programmes that address everything about the child that is autistic, it's far better to let the child help with the decision. As an example, there are some mute children who want to speak. They can communicate their desire with a typing device or signing perhaps. So then, they should receive training in speech by a qualified therapist who is sensitive to the needs and idiosyncrasies of autistic little ones. As the child progresses in one chosen therapy, the parent should be assisting in private with practice sessions. Also, the parent should be teaching the child more about his condition and explaining that it is not a prison, but is rather a special brain type which results in creating a very fascinating personality. The parent must prevent the child from losing faith in herself.

In choosing a residential facility for an autistic child, the parent should always be actively participating in the child's education and living. If a parent is displeased with an aspect of the facility, no matter what it is, then she or he should speak up. Residential facilities provide supervised round-the-clock care for the child who is too much for a parent to handle in a private home. They are not places to send a child to get rid of him because you'd rather not deal with an autistic person.

Deep love is truly the best way to care for any person. The love must be eternal, deeply overflowing, respectful, fun, protective, gentle, and definitely completely non-discriminatory. As the child grows older, she will be more able to do more tasks for herself. It is up to family members to reassure her and support her. If she is constantly fuelled by love of a few close people around her, she will be stronger to face the adversity of strangers. The adversity, which must be overcome, is not the condition itself. It is the pain and limitation placed upon disabled people by non-disabled people. If a callous, ignorant individual says to someone, 'You can't do that because you're autistic', the autistic person must decide whether or not that is correct.

As mentioned before, there always is an individual variance. In one example, a non-verbal child or grown-up can't talk, whilst others can. However, there are things that are particularly autistic which almost no non-autistics can do. Apparently, the masses think they are superior because of sheer number. Yet the individual who stands alone despite the odds is stronger, and has more character than the ones who submit to allow everyone else to tell them what to do.

Autism is a lot of going your own way, doing your own thing. Nobody should be punished for that reason. If society can't accept or tolerate the many eccentricities of some people then it can simply look in another direction.

Autistics can have dreams, too. Many times it isn't the condition of Autism that holds them back and prevents those dreams from coming true, but rather it is the people and opinions around them. If autistic people don't discriminate against others for being non-autistic, then non-autistics shouldn't discriminate against special people.

§

Rhythms and Self-Stimulations

A major trait of Autism is self-stimulatory behaviour. It is an outward manifestation of a deeply inward personality. It is the trait that seems to irritate outsiders. It attracts attention and rude comments. Some parents and schoolteachers strive to eliminate a child's self-stimulations. This is, in my opinion, wrong to do.

Self-stimulation is connected to emotions and senses. Autistic people are famous for their self-stimulatory actions. There are countless varieties of them. The most common are body rocking, flapping the hands, head bobbing, swaying from side to side, gazing at the hands, and making various sounds. Some others involve rubbing and touching the skin with an object and tasting or smelling everything, including people, and tapping everything.

Deeply autistic people create stimulations with many things they come across. They will many times be performing a task and a self-stimulation at the same time. Some physicians explain how a living being needs stimulation. When it doesn't get it, it will create its own. Self-stimulatory behaviours are observed in caged animals, as well as domesticated animals who become bored, such as horses in stalls. They amuse themselves by certain movements. Therefore, professionals sometimes claim that when a child with Autism is forced to engage in activities of the big world, the self-stimulations will diminish. My question is, so what if they are there in the first place?

I happen to have many self-stimulatory behaviours. I love them and enjoy them. I affectionately call them my 'stimmies'. Autistic people generally do enjoy their stimulations. They are comforted by them, and are relaxed by them. They may be embarrassing to parents or others, but they are pleasant for the autistic one, so they must be allowed to be a part of the whole person.

Some stimmies create an interesting picture of the world. Through self-stimulations the child can explore. Many children spin their bodies round and round and round. They have a different equilibrium, so they don't become dizzy the way that non-autistics will. Also, the sensation of dizziness can please an autistic child. These children do play, contrary to what the books often say. Their play is repetitive, comfortable, and involves a lot of self-stimulation. Jumping is another exploratory stimulation. Leaping into air feels exhilarating. A child with Autism will find an action which feels good, then repeat it with much more perseverance than a regular child.

Autistics are captivated by movements and inner rhythms. They can become absorbed inside their own body rhythms – digestion, heart beat, swallowing, or breathing. These provide a stabilizing action, which grounds the child who is deeply within himself. These children are quite pre-occupied with themselves. They focus upon some point of themselves to help calm them especially when they are threatened.

Self-stimulations aren't a behaviour problem. They shouldn't be disciplined. Those which are self-injurious, can be re-directed into more gentle actions. Body rocking whilst sitting is probably the stimmy that most people who know anything at all about Autism are familiar with. Rocking connects one with one's inner music. It is connected with a very deep, primitive way of being soothed. Autistics retain a connection to their innermost deep selves. They are guttural, emotional people. Being primitive is not negative. It is pure and honest, rather uninfluenced by the outside world.

Actually, a parent can feel closer to the child by getting involved with his self-stimulations. No words need to be uttered. You can just quietly sit and rock with the child, or follow the child, doing what he is doing. The child may seem remote from you, but actually will be pleased. You're making an effort to participate in activities of his own world. He can trust you better now. You both can play at being mirrors to one another. See who initiates movements first. This is a way to experience a basic relationship with your child. This technique can be used by friends, siblings, therapists, and doctors. There is nothing idiotic or embarrassing about imitating the stimmies of an autistic person. It is an act of caring, unless it is done in mockery. It is an act of learning more about someone you care for by experiencing what he is experiencing. This is what the goal should be. The goal should not be to eventually draw the child 'out' into the big world, because it just may not be best. It's interesting that no matter what they always retain their inner worlds. They can learn to have control over what or who enters their world to enrich their experiences.

People surrounding the person with Autism can also be enriched. By observing the initially alien actions of this mysterious person, non-autistic people can learn to appreciate. They will gradually become less fearful of what is different. This is like studying the customs of a different culture. It is like learning a different language.

Sometimes the type of self-stimulations change or lessen as the person grows up. Other times new stimulations replace old ones. The intensity can also even increase with age. Usually, the individual will seem to prefer a group of stimmies that favour a specific sensory channel. Children who are rockers often also are hand-flappers. They enjoy movements and rhythms. Of course, many children can be seen performing many kinds of stimulations. Often the child will run past a stationary object, peeking at it as he races by. He is intrigued by the way its appearance is changed by his own movement. He is exploring his environment, learning about spatial relations, enjoying physical sensations. Autistic children seem to like just wandering about. They will choose a certain route then walk it all around the house. In times of high anxiety, they will probably pace rapidly to and fro.

Self-stimulations come naturally from early on. They can be a way to burn away nervous energy, too. Autistics are highly excitable people. When regular methods of trying to calm themselves fail, they usually can get relief from self-stimulations. Trying to get them to give up their stimmies for another way of comfort that is more acceptable can be painful and is viewed as a threat. The only reason autistic stimulations aren't acceptable to the big world is because the big world is too easily embarrassed. The big world also has a vicious stigma against anybody with a mental illness or a different mental function. Autism isn't mental illness. Yet, for some reason, people call autistics crazy, nutty, daft, and weird. People allow themselves to be embarrassed. Nobody can really make another person feel embarrassed unless that person allows it to happen.

Adults can actually cause harm when they try to stop a child's stimulations. They might touch the child or loudly reprimand. These are two acts which will unfailingly startle the child. There is no reason to reprimand a child for indulging in self-stimulatory behaviours. Almost all stimmies are harmless and enjoyable.

The exception is the self-abusive child. This is a rare occurrence. But it is frightening. Yet is has its reasons. Self-abuse can be caused by several things:

1. In times of terribly gripping anxiety, the child may bite and smack herself. She seems not to feel the pain. Actually, she minds the pain much less than she would if another person did the same thing to her. Because of sensory delicacies, the mere pat of another's hand can startle her and make her screech in emotional alarm. Emotional pain can be totally devastating. So she reaches for help inside herself – a very natural thing for her to do. She smacks herself in the face. Now her attention is drawn wholly upon herself. She can better shut out whatever intrusion has just occurred. Also, causing abrupt physical pain jogs the brain to quickly release dopamine, a natural chemical sedative.

2. A seriously self-abusive youngster can be the result of trapped frustration and rage. The non-verbal child (the most severely self-abusive individuals are almost always non-verbal) may be wrestling with inner language and the formidable communication gaps between herself and others. There is so much inside an autistic child. If none of it can come out, the child will be close to erupting. Patiently working with the child teaching a form of communication – either speech or something else – will most likely help her to relax. Some of her rage will then be able to be released. She will begin to understand the motives of a few very kind people, so they won't seem so much of a threat. She can learn the names of her profoundly swelling emotions. Music can help tremendously in an instance like this because music is a language and an eloquent expression. That will take

advantage of most autistic people's innate love and feel for music.

3. Take notice of the times when the child becomes self-abusive. In most cases it will occur in a burst. Sometimes to an outsider, the reason may not be apparent. The reason may originate in a hidden private part of the inner world. Many times, self-abusive outbursts are the result of intense displeasure. Since autistics sense the emotions of others, they can become quite at a loss when they feel others disapprove of them. To them, they don't really know what it is that is so wrong. They are not naughty. They don't want to hurt or upset anybody. They can grow very upset when their parent is cross with them. Especially as they grow into their teens, emotions become turmoil. They may become more self-abusive. As regular changes occur in their bodies at puberty (autistic children are not immune to this) they react with a short temper and confusion. They may feel remorse and dislike themselves. Striking back, they can wound themselves. They can be taught by disapproving others to hate themselves. Of course, that is dangerous and very wrong.

4. Self-abuse can be caused by fear and anger when a child is punished. The child actually has no idea why the parent punishes her. If a child wanders past a vase while doing a certain self-stimulation involving hands, and knocks the vase to the floor, it is an accident. Many autistic body movements are involuntary. They can be set off by becoming immersed in delicious sensory stimulations. Autistic people can be seen happily shivering when their stimmies swell large to consume them. That's the same as when a dog quivers smilingly as he enjoys someone's fingers, scratching him at the most perfect spot along his spine. It is a deeply sensuous feeling. It's a safe, happy sensation of warm waves flowing up and outward.

Many children (and also grown-ups) with Autism masturbate a lot. It feels good. They should never be punished for doing it. Never tell a child she is bad for doing any self-stimulatory behaviour. Never shout, 'Stop that!' That will only baffle and hurt the child. Plus, it is cruel to try to take away something somebody loves and has fun doing.

I am against using drugs for autistic people. The medications prescribed for people who are this way are potentially dangerous and sometimes addictive. Children who have seizures can benefit from various types of therapy. They also may be helped with a natural food substance called dimethylglycine (usually called, simply, DMG).

DMG is a relative of the B-complex vitamins. It can be purchased in health food stores. It comes in wee, white round tablets, which have a mildly sweet taste and are easily dissolved in the mouth. Many parents experiment with DMG to discover how it affects their child. It has been reported to have so-called miracle effects, such as helping non-verbal children begin speaking overnight. It has also been reported to lessen outbursts of rage or self-abuse, or self-stimulations.

I'm sceptical of anything that is said to have a miracle effect. I also believe that Autism should not be tampered with even by natural means, unless there is a blatant serious problem that is causing the child pain, such as seizures or severely self-abusive behaviour. I'm against professionals or parents administering any substance to the child in hopes of simply diminishing autistic behaviour. But, at least DMG won't harm the child, and if he is very angry and aggressive, then it is indeed worth a try. If you decide to try DMG, do remember to store the tablets in the foil packaging they come inside. Each tablet is packaged individually for a reason: DMG is highly water-soluble and if a tablet is set out overnight, and the air is humid, it will dissolve completely away into nothing. Also, if any liquid is spilled on a tablet, it will immediately begin to melt.

Some self-stimulations are subtle. They can include gazing at the hands, staring at a dot of sunshine on the carpet, visually following movements, or simply watching the glow of shining objects. These are also comforting, relaxing actions. They reflect a safe place deep inside, rather like a form of meditation.

§

NINE

Relationships

Because of the social and communication differences in Autism, relationships can be very difficult. Some of the problems will be explained here, as well as how it feels from many autistic people's point of view.

It probably isn't possible for any autistic to have a so-called normal relationship with anybody. Relationships involve emotions and allowing another person to come close to you. A major stumbling block to regular relationships is the fact that the other person is outside the autistic world. Even to get involved with another autistic is to get involved with a separate person who isn't you.

Autistic children can feel close to their families. They can have a special love as long as things are gentle and non-threatening. They enjoy being with people they feel secure around. They can become quite attached to those who are kind and who protect them, and are patient and caring. They certainly are capable of loving their parents and receiving love, although it can be a very unusual, unique love. There is a refreshing purity and innocence about autistic people.

In friendships autistic individuals desire the same virtues that regular people probably would like: honesty, patience, caring, and consistency. Autistics tend to take things to extremes, including fears, obsessions, likes, and all their personality traits. Sometimes they do actually react the same way as other people do, only their reactions are much more pronounced.

An interesting barrier to relationships is the autistic need for sameness in the environment. That includes surrounding people! An autistic person is confused by other people's actions. She is disturbed by their unpredictability. Any time that you respond to, approach, or deal with another, you don't know what that other will do. That risk is too great for an autistic to take. Because autistics think so differently from non-autistics, there is a natural separation between them. That doesn't actually have to be a bad thing. It's rather like a cultural difference between people of different nations. Some people who grew up in Europe and are very immersed in a European way of life, may be startled, confused, overwhelmed by moving to Vietnam – especially if the individual doesn't speak Vietnamese. An acclimatization process occurs, however, so in time, the European takes on the Vietnamese way of life.

That does not happen with an autistic, except occasionally superficially. An autistic person can learn to mimic others, but never truly grows to understand why they do what they do. So I feel it is foolish to try to make someone mimic others. It makes no sense.

Autistics are content within themselves. Their own souls must give them comfort, since so much of what is outside them doesn't regularly give them the comfort they need. They are meticulous in arranging their world. They gather and catalogue the objects that are part of their world tightly about themselves. Whenever bringing a new object into their experience, they purify it, make it acceptable to be a portion of themselves. Then it feels safe enough to enrich their realm. That can't be done with people. People keep changing. They have their own personal wills and minds. They are terribly unpredictable. They usually aren't trying to hurt the autistic person, but their sheer differences and unpredictability can be intolerable.

One way to ease that is to explain your actions to the autistic person. Preparing her for your actions lessens the shock of the unknown. Telling her how certain things make you feel can help both of you grow closer. Autistics need someone to trust, and they also need to trust themselves. As with parenting, love and patience are the most crucial ingredients for a friendship. A person can be a good friend to an autistic child or grown-up by including the special one in activities. Large parties or outings that involve mobs of people are probably a bad idea. But peaceful gatherings of family and friends can indeed be enjoyed. Disabled people should not be shunned. They should not be kept out of holiday and birthday celebrations. Loving people who surround them can overlook their autistic eccentricities. The ideal environment is one where both autistic and non-autistic individuals feel confident and free to be themselves. Harmony can be achieved by everyone respecting each other.

Autistics aren't the only ones who are limited. Everybody has limitations. It's just that the limitations are different, and some people's limitations stand out more than others do.

An autistic person feels afraid and chaotic when he's not in control. An equal give and take in a relationship probably isn't possible. The autistic one may understand that there is a lot of giving in a relationship. But he most likely will see it as impossible not to take more than he gives. Giving so much to another involves very strong emotions that tend to overwhelm. It also involves being attentive to the other person's thoughts. That also is difficult because the autistic is self-absorbed and centred on himself. He's not deliberately viciously selfish. But he is within himself and doesn't easily feel the other person. He can't disrupt his own safe way of living to adopt anyone else's.

The things mentioned above are facts, which an autistic can learn and remember. It is the action and the emotion that goes along with it all that often proves to be too much. There can be relationships; only they must be unique, not measured against any others.

Autistics can be devastated, yet not cry. They can react wildly to events others treat as trivial. They can, and do, miss loved ones who have died. They can be deeply scarred for years following the loss of someone they feel attached to. Not only have they lost someone they enjoyed being around, their routine has been altered, as well, so they feel afraid. Their attachments come from a very deep, primitive source. It connects to their unrefined emotions that are very like an animal's, as stated in a previous chapter.

The autistic mourning process is close to that of an animal's. As swans and lovebirds and parrots pine for their mate who has passed away, autistics feel the same sense of destruction. There have been stories of wolves who have died of a broken heart when their mates were killed. Also, in the close-knit family-oriented elephant herd, survivors have been filmed tarrying over the bones of a deceased family member, as if to bid farewell.

Even if the reader does not share the author's deep respect and love for the animal kingdom, and does not agree that the animals are full of intelligence and dignity, there are striking similarities between autistic people and animal behaviour that need to be studied. There are tremendous similarities, actually, between all people and animal behaviour, because humans are also animals.

Many autistic children and adults find it easier to become attached to animals than to become attached to people. Sometimes, however, autistic children are frightened of animals. Animals are often unpredictable, just as humans are. Some of them can also make very loud sounds, which startle the highly sensitive autistic child who dislikes a lot of noise. Autistics and animals are deeply intuitive and they sense things most people miss. There probably is a kind of sixth sense associated with Autism. Of course, that has nothing to do with anything of the occult or demonic, although there are still people who insist it has.

A lot goes on beneath the surface of an autistic person, which is not all exposed. Events of the big world can traumatize an autistic child. Loss of anything beloved is one of these events. So it is important to minimize the occurrence of things such as this.

Again, I stress communication. Whether it be by spoken words, or signing, typing or writing, or pointing to pictures, whether it be by body language, joyous laughter, tears, or bolting, the autistic individual will definitely benefit from a release of the emotions associated with any type of relationship. If the friend, parent, or carer takes the precious time to help, to listen and to explain events, it will lessen tears and pains. The autistic emotions easily become jumbled so the person doesn't know what the hell is going on. If a trusted friend stays near, that will do a great deal to provide consistency and compassion, two things an autistic person needs. That is also a part of a relationship.

Autistics can also be good friends. Parents are often comforted simply by the silent presence of their child, even if the child is non-verbal. In relationships, there are many things that can only be felt. They can't be proven by science. A great deal in Autism can't be proven by the doctors or researchers – so it must be explained by the autistic people themselves. Each one who is capable of some sort of voice deserves to be heard (or seen, or read). Knowing this spurs each relationship to grow closer. The non-autistic partner in the relationship must approach the autistic one with love and respect and must never treat the other as inferior. This holds true even for those autistics who are non-verbal and also said to be severely mentally retarded.

Relationships are real, no matter if they are complicated or simple. Anything can be used as a stepping block for forming a relationship. Art and music are superb for that. It must never be forgotten that the child will remain autistic, even if he changes from unreachable to engaging. Many autistics are charming, wonderful people who would make nice friends to others. A parent of a non-autistic child shouldn't refuse to allow his or her youngster to play with an autistic boy or girl. The autistic generally shies away from playing with other chilren. One reason is that other children are separate individuals who are unpredictable and can confuse the special-needs child.

One step is to approach the autistic person on his own level. If he is a non-verbal person who can read and write, write him a hello note. Always go at his own pace, not yours. Always invite the withdrawn child to participate in activities, but don't force him. Autistic people are quite capable of feeling deep loneliness. But they also favour being by themselves a lot. Not all of them are lonely, either.

Use things the autistic individual enjoys to spark her interest. If she likes music and hums to herself, use music as an introduction to relating to other people. It is a falsehood that autistics do not relate. Rather, they relate in their own ways.

You cannot force or trick an autistic child. They almost always will see straight through it and know what you're up to. Then they will lose trust in you. Relationships must be honest and pure. The autistic person needs to be shown that she is loved just the way she is. No true, loving parent could say to a child, 'If you weren't autistic, I would love you more'.

I am frankly irritated by the current uproar over diagnostic terms for autistics. Autism is Autism. If it is mild, moderate, or severe, it is still Autism. If it is present in girls or boys, it is still Autism. Autism covers a wide range, a continuum. It is considered a spectrum disorder. Some doctors diagnose a child as PDD/NOS, which stands for Pervasive Developmental Disorder/Not Otherwise Specified. This label is used sometimes to designate a child who exhibits some, but not all, symptoms of autistic disorder. Sometimes it's also used as a buffer for the parents. Many parents otherwise would see the label Autism as a death sentence to their child. They have images of the non-verbal, unreachable child who never, ever learns any form of communication and spends a lifetime in an institution. That image now is gradually fading.

I use the term Autism to encompass all types of this special condition, including Asperger Syndrome. Hans Asperger was a Viennese doctor who described a bunch of seemingly autistic children. He wrote about them in 1944, a year after Leo Kanner's original description of children whom he titled 'autistic'. Dr. Asperger did not know of Kanner's work or original 1943 writings. The children Dr. Asperger met behaved very much like autistics, yet had generally very advanced speech skills and could possess highly original thought. Asperger Syndrome is thought to be less disabling overall than classical Kanner Syndrome Autism. Some professionals consider it to be a form of very able Autism (although not all highly able autistic are technically Asperger Syndrome). Some consider it to be separate from Autism. I consider it to be both. Some Asperger Syndrome individuals behave more like classical autistics; some behave more like their very own separate group.

I don't think that dividing Autism into many subgroups should serve to label the individuals. Researching Autism leads to discovering the many types, yet they all have the same characteristics at the core. 'Autism' is not a doom. It does not mean that the person will never love anyone, or is incapable of having a meaningful relationship. You have to approach an autistic a different way than other people.

Sometimes, a magical thing happens and an autistic person falls in love and even gets married. Having children is very rare, because children are generally smelly, loud, unpredictable, upset schedules, and would assault the autistic adult's sensitivities. They also require much care. Most autistic people continue to need some kind of special care continually, even if it's only emotional support. And because of the nature to be self-absorbed, it's an extremely unlikely occurrence for

them to be able to put another being – such as a child they have created – ahead of themselves.

Sometimes two special autistics meet and find happiness in each
other. An autistic can also even marry a non-autistic, as long as the latter is very patient and accepting of autistic idiosyncrasies. The spouse
must be a special person to marry another special person. Once again,
there needs to be patience and understanding, more of those two here
than in regular relationships. For it's a fact that autistic people can be
difficult to live with. Two people can meet whose personalities wrap
around one another and hug, so the people grow stronger with each
other. They can live naturally in their love. They don't need to follow
the rules of somebody else's guidebook. This wonderful occurrence
of marriage can happen not only to very mildly affected autistics. As
long as the two partners love each other, respect each other, and have
a special daily communication, as well as a way to feel safely joined,
then marriage is possible.

People with Autism indeed do know how to love. Love is an active
emotion that is innate. Parents of autistic children know and experience their child's love and even affection. Autism usually comes with
touch sensitivities. Yet affection is craved by the child with this condition. Most of them very much enjoy being caressed and carefully
hugged by people they trust. They never should be held forcefully
against their will. Each autistic one will discover his own touch preferences. As mentioned in a previous section, touch needs to be gentle
and never startling. Having respect for the child's boundaries is a
huge part of any relationship.

Protection is also greatly involved in being a friend or parent or
lover to an autistic person. The autistic is always going to be ex-
tra-sensitive, and probably also highly excitable. She will also forever
need to have her rituals and daily schedule as the structure for her life.
Her partner or family must assist in keeping her world impenetrable.
She will look to them as guardians.

Help comes in so many ways. An autistic person will look to someone close to her for help if she is coached how to approach another.
Relationships involving people who have Autism can be profound
learning experiences. Both partners can learn about each other, as
long as the goal isn't to change one another.

Parents can, and do, enjoy the company of their special child. They can learn to be friends as well as parents. They can be protective for their child's entire lifetime, and they can be someone to come to for help and affection. They can feel proud of their child, even if the child doesn't achieve success the way the big world sees it. There are many autistic people who never will get married. And there also are some non-autistic people who don't want to get married. Well, then, there will just be other kinds of relationships. Since relationships involve emotions, and emotions are free, a flowing, truthful relationship is the best kind.

One who is a true friend to an autistic will be loving, wise, and shielding. The person will strive to prevent things from frightening the autistic, and will explain events that are scary or new. The person never will make fun of the autistic one. He will be sort of a spokesperson to inform outsiders. He will be interested in the well being of the autistic. He will try to be consistent. He will be accustomed to the odd behaviours that go with being different. He won't mind being a bit embarrassed in public! He will help his special friend to make decisions, and he will be patient in communication. He will recognize the individual personality of his different friend and will find joy in it. He will assist the autistic one to become more independent and will protect him from people who only pretend to be nice.

Autistic people don't really understand how somebody could have bad intentions, yet still act friendly on the outside. That paradox is confusing for a person who needs to see things literally as they are, and not befogged with deceit. A person like this simply can't grasp how another person can be acting nice only to play tricks or to really harm the disabled individual. An autistic person can learn that things like that do happen, yet can never actually understand why they happen. An example is the author of this book, who has recorded the factual information here in this paragraph, yet has no idea how it comes to be, or any knowledge of why somebody would try to hurt somebody else! The point of this immediate paragraph is that autistics do need to be guarded from people with bad intentions. They are naive socially. Their innocence and literalness prevent them from being able to distinguish between foe or friend in many cases. And so, the people with whom they have a close relationship must do that for them. Autistic people generally don't know the things others know naturally. They can't be taken for granted, and they can't be expected to know something just because others know it. Despite the intricacy of the autistic mind, it doesn't absorb information readily unless it is open to it. So, it definitely helps for the friend to be aware of that. Of course, a true friend wouldn't insult an autistic person for not knowing something, or for using language structure that is out of place.

Siblings of autistic people need to be treated also in a special way. Classmates will make fun of them for having a weirdo or so-called 're-tard' sister or brother. Perhaps it will become difficult for them to not hate or be ashamed of the autistic. There are books that deal with that situation. Of course, all that falls into the relationship category, too. Hopefully, the non-autistic sibling will learn to look beyond other children's taunts. Brother or sister will be happier after realizing that it is not anyone's fault there is an autistic in the household. It's the tor-mentor children's problem if they cannot deal with an unusual child, or the siblings of an unusual child.

The greatest of all virtues, the most profound emotion, is love. Love sings and bounds high over clouds. If you begin any relationship with love as its steadfast nucleus, then you can be assured that you are blessed.

§

Health and Allergies

Allergies can play a large role in people with Autism. An allergy is a hypersensitivity to something that a person comes in contact with, either by touch, inhalation, or ingestion. Since autistic people are so sensitive in every aspect, it is logical that many do develop allergies, or get reactions from certain foods or things they touch.

An allergy can cause countless physical problems, emotional disturbances, and even death, as in an asthma attack, or large, dangerous hives. Generally, children with Autism don't have the life- threatening types of allergies. Pure Autism is not caused by an allergy. Some allergies, especially food intolerance, can contribute to irritability, fatigue, tantrums, odd eating habits, and overall ill feelings.

There are autistic people who don't really have allergies, and there are those who seem to react to many things. It's complicated to discover what the cause of the health change is. Parents and an allergist who is familiar with Autism can form a team to diagnose and treat food allergies. Obviously, clearing up the health disruption caused by an allergy does not clear up the Autism. It does help the autistic child or adult to feel better, however.

Sensitivities to certain fabrics can cause reactions that mimic true allergy. The mind can contribute to a lot. If an autistic boy hates the feel of wool against his skin he's going to react strongly each time he is dressed in woollens. He may not actually have a true allergy to it. But the tremendous discomfort of wool on his body upsets him. His super-sensitive skin shrieks as soon as any wool brushes it, and the fabric rubs, chafes, scratches painfully, itchingly. Nerves shoot to his brain with their danger signals. His skin responds with an eruption of hives or a rash. The boy becomes very irritable until the offensive garment is taken away. Sometimes woollen jackets can be tolerated as long as they're fully lined.

Sometimes it is ultra-smooth fabric that upsets a child. It may feel too slippery, almost wet, upon his skin. There is no point in dressing an autistic child in clothing that hurts or makes him itch. He'll only be very unhappy and will squirm to get out of it, or may whisk it off in public. He won't care that he is in a public place. He will care only that the irritant is now gone. Try to dress him in soft, comfortable clothes.

Anything at all can affect an autistic child almost like an allergy. Even a change of temperature in air currents can cause an itch on exposed skin. Some children with Autism are frequent scratchers. Gentle rubbing and scratching can become a calming self-stimulation. But when it becomes clawing, and there are rashes and open scrapes on the skin, a tactile intolerance can be responsible. Stress and anxiety also can cause skin eruptions. The mind and body are united and they greatly affect one another. An example of that is an autistic girl who is quite absorbed in herself who has spent her life creating order in her world. She rejects things of the outside, especially things that upset, frighten, threaten, or simply displease her. She is in the kitchen, preparing a sandwich for her snack. Her wooden cutting board slips from her fingers and scrapes her knee on its fall to the floor. The girl did not plan the action of dropping the board. She is surprised and her body barrier is disturbed by the board scraping past her leg, causing slight pain. The scrape is mild. But she was slightly assaulted from the outside. So, when she bends to pick the board up, she notices the large pink welt on her knee. Her skin – the largest sense organ – has reacted in self-protection and shock. She may recover faster than it takes for the welt to go down.

This kind of thing can also happen with bites and stings of insects. The welt may remain longer and the child may keep scratching until it bleeds. That's another assault – how dare that mosquito cross the autistic barrier? Make certain the non-verbal autistic child is supervised when playing outside in pleasant weather. The child could be stung and develop a serious allergic reaction, and wouldn't be able to tell someone what happened, of course. Also, a lot of autistic children develop a self-stimulatory behaviour called pica, which means they eat non-food items, including something that could poison them.

Eating involves the body accepting items outside it. It can be very difficult for an autistic to accept anything from the outside. Eating can also become self-stimulatory. There is no way an autistic child is going to eat something she hates, or doesn't like the feel of. I believe everyone, autistic or non-autistic, should take a daily multi-vitamin, multi-mineral. Autistic children or adults who are extremely finicky diners must be sure to do this.

One symptom of a food allergy is that the individual craves the very same food he is allergic to. Perhaps that is an attempt by the body to de-sensitize itself, as in homeopathic medicine. Also, people who must receive injections for their seasonal allergies get minute amounts of their personal allergens added to their serum. This, of course, serves to acclimate the immune system so it no longer treats the substance as foreign, then it no longer attacks itself.

In true cases of food allergy, however, eating the problem food doesn't have the same affect – actually, it could kill you. In hypersensitive autistics, the problem foods must be eliminated until symptoms disappear. Sometimes the foods can be re-introduced in small amounts, then increased gradually. Once the immune system is healed and stabilized, it can happen that the foods can again be tolerated. Allergies can come and go. Stress can also wear the entire body down, making the problem foods more of an irritant. In times of stress the mind and body should be comforted and well-nourished with gentle, healthful foods. The individual should get enough rest and sleep, too. Balance is important.

In Autism, things usually happen in extremes. Autistics have very strong preferences. They have strong likes and dislikes, and are actually passionate. So, it's more natural for them to react in extremes. If they like whole grain bread, for an example, they may try to eat an entire loaf.

Some of the foods which cause allergies in many autistic children are wheat, yeast, MSG, milk, and aspartame. Aspartame is an interesting sweetener that has disturbing affects on some non-autistic people, as well. It is made from natural substances. However, the substances combined do not exist in nature, and that in itself can sometimes cause problems. People have reported digestive disturbances, headaches, and depression as a result of regularly ingesting aspartame. It could be a prime problem for sensitive autistic people. In my opinion, all artificial flavourings and colourings and preservatives should be eliminated from the autistic's diet. I do not like the idea of feeding anybody something unnatural. The bodies of many autistic children also do not like the idea.

MSG (monosodium glutamate) comes from soy. It is used as a preservative and flavour-enhancer, especially in some Chinese restaurants, and in packaged foods. It is of course always listed on the supermarket labels. I suggest the autistic child be kept away from it. It is basically harmless in people who have no sensitivity to it. But it is not a necessary ingredient and can make highly sensitive individuals ill.

Phenylalanine is a natural substance, too. It is an amino acid. Some people are born with a genetic inability to metabolise phenylalanine in their brains. This condition is called phenylketonuria (PKU) and is tested for at birth. If a phenylketonuric eats a food that contains phenylalanine, it will build to a toxic level in the brain. Some autistics have this disease, which is a mental retardation syndrome.

Of course an individual can be allergic to anything. The general public sometimes over-reacts to the so-called link between Autism and food allergy. They grope desperately about for a cure, or for some magic that will make the person's Autism less noticeable. There is a lot of quackery in the allergy profession. Again, I stress that Autism is nobody's fault. It is not brought on by a food allergy, or by malnutrition. It is not caused by a parent's failure to feed a child properly. Some people simply are much more sensitive to everything than others are. So, if there is a specific food that is very harsh, or is liable to cause stomach upset, then the autistic child may be unable to tolerate it.

Wheat is one food that can be heavily laden with pesticides. Even organic wheat may produce discomfort in people who react to the plant itself. Wheat can make allergic rhinitis symptoms worse. It also can cause some disturbances of the gastrointestinal tract. It can cause allergy shiners, the darkened circles beneath the eyes. In most cases, it probably is not a true allergy, but more of a sensitivity.

There is a great deal of talk and writings concerning yeast and Autism. Many doctors and parents claim that the traits of Autism are much more pronounced after ingesting anything that contains yeast or molds. This doesn't include only breads and other baked goods, but all grains except rice, millet, and quinoa, as well as any item which tends to attract spores of mold, such as dried fruits. Pickled foods also can't be eaten because yeast lives in vinegar. Various sugars must be avoided, too. So must many condiments and spices.

Candidiasis is real. But most people who are thought to have it, don't. So many parents leap at the chance that a candida (yeast) infection or intolerance may be the reason the child is autistic. They eliminate a huge number of foods from the child's diet. In the case of an autistic who is most likely a picky eater anyway, it's ridiculous to put the child through that ordeal. A completely mold and yeast-free diet is indeed boring and can be very traumatic to the child with Autism, in true candidiasis the person has almost always suffered from other, more localized yeast infections, such as diaper rash, or thrush. Another factor to contribute to candida intolerance is an infection that requires a lengthy treatment of antibiotics.

Diagnosis of candidiasis must be done by a physician. Candidiasis can contribute to other allergies, as well, since the immune system is taxed. Observing the child's overall health will yield much information. Energy levels, eye brightness, skin colour, are things that can help diagnose problems such as food or chemical intolerance. Just because a child has Autism doesn't mean she is in poor health. Many autistics, especially those with classic Kanner type Autism, are exceptionally healthy. Autism is not automatically connected with severe allergies and terrible health. Too much emphasis on that is taking away from what Autism really is.

It could be considered that autistics are allergic to the world! They are hypersensitive to so many things, both in their environment and within their bodies. That is not a terrible thing, though. It can be a tremendous gift. It roots them in nature. It is part of being a live organism who thinks, breathes, cries, eats, dances, sings with life, and searches for the beauty all around. Autistic people are even very sensitive to changes in weather and time changes. It's at the point of being overwhelmed that it can feel as if you're allergic to everything. Being 'allergic' to people is not difficult, especially if the particular people are uncaring or intensely frightening, so sometimes the autistic one's reaction appears much like a strong allergy.

Being in a state of high anxiety where every sense is heightened, and every nerve is jangling can make someone act irritated. Some things may make someone act in a bizarre way (bizarre compared to regular people) in response to a stimulus. So reactions can seem like allergies on the surface. Actual allergies aren't made up. If one does have them, they obviously cause that autistic individual unhappy discomfort, sometimes to an extreme degree.

Dealing with allergies should always engage a professional, someone who is no less than an expert. Things affect autistics in different ways than they affect non-autistics. Medicines should be used only when completely necessary and they must be used with great care. A natural treatment should always be tried first. In the instance of a severe asthma attack, however, a vitamin or herb is not going to work!

Allergies are often complicated to discover, and can be elusive. Autism doesn't cause the allergy, so the condition must not be blamed.

Health is an interesting portion of Autism. Autistic children can be taught to keep themselves tidy. Self-cleanliness is crucial to good health. That becomes a large problem in children who play with their pee and poop. To them those aren't dirty. They don't realize that it can make them sick. They have a fascination for anything that comes out of their body. It's again a question of where the self ends and the outside begins. Some children do that to mark their territory with something their body has created. It makes things of the outside more acceptable and safe to them.

Technically, body waste material is not a horrible, filthy thing; but rather a natural process. The fact that, in sick individuals, waste can spread infection and is the toxic remains of food and liquids, is what makes it all seem awful and yucky. Perhaps it would help to not be shocked when an autistic child spreads turds all over the wall as a natural painting. It will help to find out his reason for doing it. If he is experimenting, get him paper and washable paints. If he is branding the outside world so it isn't as frightening to him, help him discover a new way to do that. Autistic children aren't deliberately vicious. There occasionally is a bit of naughtiness in seeing what reaction the child can get from other people, but that can be a way of trying to communicate, too.

It's quite helpful to be aware of all the details in the health of an autistic child or grown-up. Autism affects many, many things from perception to thought patterns, metabolism, sensitivities, ability to learn in a traditional way, temperament, ability to focus, memory, language, and social styles. I consider it a marvellous gift to be so sensitive, so attuned to the rhythms of nature and my inner body. Actually, when a stimulus hurts or overwhelms, it is mostly a stimulus that is either harmful or harsh, anyway; only most non-autistic people don't have a big reaction to it. For example, fluorescent light isn't exactly a pleasant environment for anybody. Food additives aren't healthful for anyone, either. An environment of noise and confusion will sap anyone's peace. It is simply that autistic people reach their threshold of tolerance much sooner. They really need to feel balanced, which is only natural.

§

ELEVEN

Autism and Teenage Years

Since people with Autism are innately much more sensitive than non-autistic people, puberty can be extremely difficult. The non-autistic young teenager experiences changes within his or her body and goes through emotional tidal waves. The same things happen to autistic children, too. Those changes and resulting turmoil often make the young person very difficult. Tantrums basically will increase. Rage reactions may become very out of control. The child himself will be feeling overwhelmed and frightened also, so he is definitely not trying to harm anyone else.

School problems can erupt at this special time. Changes in puberty are exciting and they represent a beautiful blooming of a new young adult person inside. The transition will be made smoother if the autistic teen is comforted and given tons of support from her family. Society can contribute to self-loathing of the teenager, even in non-autistics. There is too much pressure put upon teenagers. Also there is too much peer competition. It is not the individual boy's fault when his voice cracks as it adjusts to its new timbre. It is not the young lady's fault if she develops large boobs years before the rest of the girls. Those things are up to nature and heredity. But if those things occur to an autistic youngster who is already regularly taunted by classmates, it will all be made worse by adding more reason for tormentors to torment. Some people will pick on anything. Teenagers who are feeling quite insecure try to make themselves feel better by being cruel to someone else, especially a person who sticks out from crowds.

Tormenting can easily cause the sensitive child to hate the part of himself that draws negative attention. That is a tragic thing. Nobody should hate himself. And surely there is no reason to hate your own body as it prepares for a new stage in life. This is a time to celebrate life. The new teenager is learning about himself. He is growing without and within. He is questioning, and getting answers leading to more questions. He shouldn't be ashamed to question. As autistics generally are more naive than other peers, they often get laughed at if they ask simple questions. That has nothing to do with intelligence, or lack of it. Being naive is not being stupid. Yet that is what he is called because he may not know how babies are created.

Autistic teenagers do have stirrings sexually within them. They can become interested in the other sex. They do not know how to approach members of the other sex. They can be coached gently on how they can do so. Yet they also must be allowed to be themselves and they will always be different.

It is essential to teach some sex education to autistic teenagers; especially those who are more advanced. If they have an interest in having a girlfriend or boyfriend, that desire is very real and very lovely, and should never be scoffed at. Autistic people do have morals. They can get a clear, solid understanding of right and wrong. Autistic people make deeply loyal friends. They have an ability to share their lives with someone who is trusted and loved. They don't necessarily have to have a girlfriend or boyfriend or spouse, who is also autistic, yet that may happen. If the autistic teenager wants to have a love relationship, he needs to be educated about how babies are made and what can happen if sexual intercourse is done hastily or with an ill-suited partner. Sexually transmitted diseases must be discussed. The dangers of AIDS must be outlined. Everything must be presented without overwhelming emotions. Facts must be presented very clearly. Then the teenager with Autism will remember and apply that information.

If a family has certain religious beliefs, or moral beliefs, then those should also be discussed. However, keep in memory that the teenager is not the parent. The teenager is her own person. Autistic teenagers can be rebellious. Their rebellion is a form of communication and self-discovery. If they use an argument, 'Nobody understands me', they're right. They need someone who will take the time to understand, not condemn.

Autistic teenagers live more sheltered lives than others, usually, and they do enjoy being on their own a lot. They can make their own decisions. They understand when an issue is major, such as sex. They should be trusted to make some of their own judgements. Even in the case of a less advanced autistic teenager who isn't going to be interested in getting a boyfriend or girlfriend, she still needs her own space and life. No child, either autistic or non-autistic, is born to be an extension of the parents. No child is meant to carry the terrible burden of being expected to fulfil someone else's dreams. Children do not belong to anyone.

Autistic teenagers who see their classmates going on dates may tend to feel left out of something. There are also autistic teenagers who don't care if they are excluded, who are more interested in their own solitary pursuits. The latter was a description of myself. There is nothing wrong with being either type. There is nothing sinfully 'abnormal' about never being interested in marriage or dating.

Parents can provide guidance (not dictatorship) concerning the autistic young adult's romance. A wonderful, loving mate can be a profoundly beautiful experience for an autistic teenager. Most of them are intellectually advanced, yet emotionally retarded. Being paired with a special girlfriend or boyfriend can be a magical release and freedom. Both will learn about themselves together.

Autistics are not superficial people. They are intense and deep. They innately know what counts most in a relationship. As they grow into their teenage years they have strong emotions to sort out. Some of their obsessions will seem more powerful, whilst some may change or disappear. If they were always difficult to handle, they probably will become even more difficult.

In girls, hygiene is very crucial when they begin to menstruate. They also can have painful periods and PMS. Their bodies are already attuned to inner details, and they are sensitive. During puberty and early teenage years, they are more anxious and easily upset. Emotional turmoil can cause problem periods and irregularities. Girls should be taught what menstruation is just like non-autistic females are taught. Autistic girls can take pride in caring for their bodies. To help them remember to change their spent tampons or sanitary napkins, a list can be made of simple steps to pass through, if they need it. Tampons may upset some of them because they go up into the body, which is an intrusion some don't tolerate.

If a teenage girl has menstrual problems with pain it most likely is because her Autism makes her very sensitive. She should seek treatment for the pain, because it's only made worse by her highly emotional monthly state. The pain often seems as though it radiates all over the entire body, and every nerve is screaming. That sensation is real and is nothing to scoff at. Both autistic girls and boys are quite attuned to the cycles of the moon and the rhythms of nature. So the young ladies probably have a greater chance of developing dysmenorrhoea. It's not wise to leap for a gynaecologist as the first step. An examination by a gynaecologist can be traumatic to an autistic girl especially if it is an internal. Help the girl to communicate in whatever way she can, all her symptoms to a family doctor first, or a practitioner of natural medicine.

Certain herbs for the female reproductive organs can be tried carefully. They can be combined with herbs that soothe and strengthen the nervous system. Autistic people have deeply excitable nervous systems. In a state of anxiety, pain will increase. A girl who is having intense menstrual cramps and who isn't able to tell anyone could start to hit herself or bite herself. Her body attempts to calm itself and bring itself back into balance by the brain's sudden release of dopamine. If a girl does not show any self-abuse characteristics except when she has her period, consider that as a possibility. When she is relaxed and the pain is taken away, she will feel better so that behaviour will diminish. In that case, she has used aggressive behaviour as a desperate attempt to communicate something. She should get professional help to feel better.

Any menstrual discomfort is terrible and no female should have to put up with it. The autistic teenager should find relief. She should be taught not to fear her periods and what happens inside her body at different points in her cycle. She should learn that it is a natural process and part of her own body rhythms. She needs to understand facts, so she won't end up hating her own body. Even if the girl doesn't show any direct outward signs of understanding what she is taught about this subject, tell her anyway. For just because a girl has Autism does not mean her body rhythms shut off. They simply move differently.

The fact is young autistic teenage boys and girls do suddenly become aware of their sexual organs and they do feel stirrings deep inside them, whether or not they have any concept of romance or sex. This is nothing to be embarrassed about. The youngster never, ever should be taught to be ashamed of himself or herself. That can be scarring for life.

Many autistic young people become overtly sexual. They are moved by their desires and drives – yet they're unsure of what to do with them. Masturbation usually increases at this point. That, too, is nothing shameful. It can be almost impossible to try to train an autistic person to refrain from masturbating in a public place. The child shouldn't be punished because he hasn't any concept of social behaviour. He is doing a simple, natural stimulation that feels delicious, and is born into every living animal. Sometimes explaining why you'd rather he not do it in public does get a result. But sometimes his overpowering urge is stronger than any vacant words he hears. The family and friends surrounding him can learn to overlook things like that. The autistic person means no harm. Since masturbation is not something only for children, it is wrong to shame the teenager by saying, 'You're too old for that'. The sensations that the teenager is enjoying increase as he grows well into puberty. Autistics tend to retain a child's innocence.

Rather than making a public scene whilst trying to train the teen to masturbate only at home, consider helping him (or her) to try doing it more quietly, then, so it isn't as noticeable. The outside world cannot expect an autistic person to conform to it, just as it can't conform entirely to autistics, who are a very small minority. But society needs to learn tolerance when it comes to any type of difference. It is as simple as to say, 'Oh, she is blind, so she can't see me wave. I must say hello instead.' Autism involves much more tolerance, perhaps. It is a complete, separate personality type so maybe others find parts of it intolerable. If someone does not like a certain individual then that someone should look away, or try to appreciate why the unliked one acts the way she does. As long as the special, different individual is not severely affecting or harming anybody else, then there is no reason to condemn. Not liking the way someone dresses, moves, or eats is not a good enough excuse to condemn or taunt, or discriminate against.

Autistic behaviours tend to be accepted by others more when the child is very young. Then, when she reaches puberty and doesn't grow out of it people seem to panic. People do not grow out of Autism. That fact needs to be stressed. The autistic teenager has rights, and has inner beauties that expand, as she becomes a young adult. A child who is affectionate may become even more so as she grows up. She can be helped through difficult times by a family that is supportive. It also helps for her to look at diagrams of the changing, growing body, and to read books.

It is still a fact that there are more males with Autism than females. A boy in puberty may become quite difficult to manage. His aggression will likely increase. Yet teenage girls can also become more aggressive. A lot of it seems to be in response to increasing awareness of things happening around them. Sensing powerful displeasure or disapproval from people can make a frustrated autistic teen aggressive. Teachers and parents need to find out what is troubling the teen. As mentioned before, explaining things will help to lessen the teen's fears. Tell him that the emotional tidal waves and physical stirrings he feels are natural and healthful. Help him to appreciate himself. Help him to like the new person emerging, but also state that he still is the same in many ways. He doesn't like change.

Some autistic teenagers enjoy clothes. They may became very smart dressers. That is a good time to help teach more hygiene. When the special needs lad learns to shave, he should also be taught to keep his sexual organs clean. Sex education can sprout into an obsession in autistic teenagers just as it can in non-autistics. All autistics have a right to receive whatever education they can handle. Sex education is definitely important for them. It provides knowledge they can use to protect themselves from dishonest people who would try to take advantage of a disabled person.

Teenage years are also a time when the individual person needs to develop more of her own voice. She needs to be able to make some decisions. She needs freedom and private space, and always has needed those, and always will need them. The freedom is the freedom to be herself naturally. The space is the space to form her own life and become happily more independent. Independence comes in many forms. It is an individual issue. If an autistic person never can truly live on his own, then he can still have independence in other ways. It must be suited to each person separately. Autistics are by nature independent in ways because they live by themselves in their bubble worlds. It is the attitude of people who are closest to them that can take away some of their innate ability to strike out on their own pathway. They can quickly become dependent on someone for everything, even taking them to the bathroom. They are self-reliant in their worlds and rarely ask for comfort from somebody else. Learned helplessness comes from others who don't think they're capable of doing anything for themselves.

Autistic children are very able in many ways. They should be carefully, gently taught simple tasks so they will enjoy having the freedom to move about the house and take care of some of their own needs. Even wee autistic children can do a few little things for themselves such as deciding what they'd like on their sandwich. If they don't speak, give them a communication board and they can then point to the pictures of what they want. These tiny steps give them control over their own immediate environment in some ways. Then some of the fear of the big world lessens. They're able to get some things by themselves and they'll feel good about themselves at an early age, whilst still learning about themselves.

The particular, peculiar beauties and profound, wonderful sensitivities of the autistic realm are enriching. They don't need to become restricting. It's very easy for a disabled person to have low self-esteem.

Independence doesn't mean that every autistic adult can get a regular job and can cope with a hectic life more like that of regular people. There are other non-autistic people who can't do that, either. But independence means a lot of little, simple things. It brings with it a feeling of freedom and accomplishment. A self-sufficient child will feel proud of himself upon just making himself a sandwich. He has made it his way using fillings he has chosen. That is actually a big part of Autism: doing things in your own way, having control over your own small, private environment, making things nice for yourself, as perfectly the way your want them as possible.

Begin to help the autistic child to do some things independently very early. As events progress, the child will turn into a teenager and will feel better about himself for being able to do small tasks without intervention. Don't compare his abilities to other teenagers. Don't use any statements that will make him feel less than his peers. Just because they started learning to drive a car doesn't mean he must, also. If he does want to, that is possible. Some autistics can drive. It's not always the most advanced who do so, or the only mildly autistic ones. If one wants to drive, and can handle it, then he should have that opportunity. His driving can be limited for safety, yet he can still do it. Perhaps another person must ride with him. Perhaps he can't tolerate driving at night because of the glaring lights. Yet that doesn't mean he can never drive at all.

As a teenager the autistic individual wonders about many things. She may ask questions that only a much younger child would ask. Questions aren't foolish, they show interest. They deserve answers.

Some parents find that their child becomes impossible to cope with in teenage years. When everything else is tried but fails, the young person may benefit from living in a residential facility where he will be given supervision and education. Those places are *not* asylums. They are places better equipped for handling extremely difficult individuals. I believe residential placement should be done only when all else doesn't work. I believe the best place for an autistic child or teenager is the home. Not all severely autistic people are also severely difficult. It is quite an individual trait. If the teenager needs to move into a special home, the parent hasn't failed at being a good parent. The parent should not feel guilty! What you are really doing is putting the child into a new home, a place where she will receive care and have access to doctors, as well as getting schooling. She may even be able to leave the facility in the future.

Get professional help to choose a residential school for your child. Go to visit the place and bring the child or teenager. If something seems suspicious about the place, don't send your son or daughter there. Be certain in all cases that you will be able to keep informed of the child's life there. You have not stopped being the parent of that individual person. You simply are enlisting assistance from professionals who can help ensure that the autistic person gets excellent loving care, and has opportunities to have a pleasant, fulfilling life. Of course even if someone is seriously mentally retarded and doesn't seem to be able to partake of a regular lifestyle it does not mean he can't still feel happy and fulfilled. Many times an autistic child will spend teenage years in a residential school then will be able to move elsewhere when he reaches his early twenties.

Obviously make sure the facility is reputable and recommended by top physicians in the field. If any medications are routinely used by staff to 'control' the behaviour of residents, *do not* put your child in their care. Again I stress, residential schools for special children are not asylums. The children are not treated as though they are dangerously mentally ill. That is a completely separate thing, yet the public does not often know that.

Good residential facilities have a staff that is truly loving, caring, and treats each child or young adult as a precious individual with potential and gifts. Do stay involved. Interact closely with the staff. You may also bring your child home for visits. The facilities are not prisons. If one you visit feels eerily like that, leave immediately. Many young autistics enjoy their residential facilities. They appreciate the structured days. They sense they are safe, and well cared for. This can relieve the person's family to enjoy more outings and freedom. They may even occasionally take the special child along with him.

No child, teenager, or grown-up tries to become a burden upon anyone. The teen years are a time of big natural changes. Surrounding people need to be aware of the special autistic sensitivities that will alter those regular changes. The growing autistic person needs to be loved and accepted, celebrated. The passage of stages in the person's life should be as happy and exciting as can be.

§

TWELVE

Recreation

There are many things autistic people can enjoy. Children with Autism can't waste away youth working in therapy programmes. They need to play a lot, and are able to play, contrary to what some books say. They usually enjoy running and rolling and tumbling about. They are fascinated to look at objects upside down and whilst rushing past them. They spin rapidly as a self-stimulation, and get a natural high by the numb soaring sensation they feel upon stopping. As they're spinning, that vast outside of chaos is reduced to a layered blur. The fear is reduced, too.

Many games help the child to develop better co-ordination. Autistic children often like the same games other children like. They tend to be thrilled with the sensation of flying through space; especially flying combined with rhythm, such as swinging. Many are highly graceful. They may also have a few areas of uncoordinated movements, however, as though disconnected. They frequently like climbing and do so without fear.

Physical fitness is important. It is very good for autistic people to get exercise. Actually, some self-abusive behaviour comes out of frustrated boredom. Exercise provides a channel for trapped energy to be released. Running, jumping, whirling, are all wonderful releases. As the child grows older, she may do well riding a bicycle, if she has the co-ordination to do so. Autistic little ones should get some exercise every day. It can even be just dancing to music. People with Autism aren't sickly and deprived of muscle tone unless they lead that kind of sedentary life. They like to be active. They may also have periods of hypoactivity along with hyperactivity. They can become scared to move lest they disturb something, or knock something awry, either literally, or inside themselves. They need the space to play freely without obstructions. If they prefer to play in solitude, then someone can just hover nearby to offer protection. But they also can enjoy playing with another person.

Here is one idea: approach a child softly, and tell him that you'd like to play with him. Then wait nearby to allow him to choose what he wants to do next. It's best to not watch him closely, as he could be upset by feeling direct eye-contact, but, to rather look busy with something else. Periodically let him know you're still interested. It could take a while, but he may decide to inch nearer and attempt to engage you in his activity.

It will help to insert playtimes and exercise times into slots in the child's daily schedules. Things must have a structured routine for an autistic to feel safe and in control. It can help a child who can read to list the activities of the daily routine. Then, perhaps, sometimes there can be a blank spot left for the child to fill in with a desired activity.

Some autistic people like to go shopping. They are attracted by bright objects and like to touch the fabrics of clothing. They like to look in windows of shops. They may bolt, however, so they need to be supervised. They could wander off and wouldn't seem too upset about being temporarily misplaced. They get their minds set on something that attracts them, and then they're off! Others are more timid, clinging to their parent's hand. Although they're fascinated by all the exciting colours and things to see and movements to watch, they're also deliciously overwhelmed and prefer to keep safely close to a protector. If someone says hello to them, they try to disappear. The sensation of being looked at, the feeling of existing is too much for them to handle. These children would do better with quiet types of recreation: walks in a forest park, horse riding, swinging, running along the ocean. It is a good idea to keep autistic people away from fluorescent lighting. Some have a strong sensitivity to it and their eyes become pink, they become restless, fussy, and may cry tiredly. If an autistic child spends a short time in a place with fluorescent lighting, and is already worn out and whining, do consider that possibility. That type of lighting is glaring and very harsh. Also, some light fixtures can emit an agonizing continuous hum that the sensitive ears of an autistic child will detect. The lights can affect an autistic grown-up in the same way. They make the nerves hurt!

Autistic children can enjoy nature. They are often enchanted by rainbows, sunsets, clouds, butterflies, and flowers. Since they notice details, they might enjoy visiting public and private gardens. Those are lovely quiet places. They also can appreciate beaches. They may be frightened of the ocean although its roar forms a soothing rhythm. Sand is very nice to play in. A child favours scooping handfuls of sand, watching it trickle, and may do that endlessly, creating new ways to be stimulated with movement.

Therapeutic horse riding is a lovely way to help an autistic child have a fun time. Horses are marvellous, amazing creatures who have formed a beautiful partnership with the human animal. Many children and adults with disabilities love the rhythm of a horse moving

beneath them. There is the chance of achieving a union of minds: the special person's with the horse's. Riding brings joy to many. In children who have no seizures and no physical handicap, and are not afraid, their natural inner cadences and sense of balance can help them to become experienced equestrians. There are stables specifically for handicapped riders. Not every autistic person needs that type of stable. He could ride at a regular stable as long as his instructor is sensitive to his autistic needs.

Riding is exciting, and there are so many styles to choose from. Good therapeutic riding academies have a fine selection of gentle, patient horses as well as some who are spunkier. As the child grows more experienced, he can move on to better horses, better schools; even a horse of his own. A horse can be a special friend, often more so than an adult or another child. A horse isn't going to condemn or laugh at autistic behaviours. A horse isn't going to throw a rider just because he's autistic. The horse doesn't care if the rider is autistic, or white, black, Oriental, or Cherokee Indian. The deep spirits of animals are loving, wise and interested in people's personalities, not their clothes, weight, or religion. Autistics often find relationships with animals far easier than with any person. With the animal, the child can receive love and understanding attention. If the animal's actions and eyes say, 'I like you', then the child can feel assured of the truth of those feelings. Animals are not fickle or two-faced. Animals give love all of the time, not only when their autistic friend pleases them.

However, some animals can tend to get a bit pushy and may not quite appreciate the autistic boundaries, such as many dogs. Pets must be chosen with the autistic child in mind. She must feel comfortable and accepting of the new family member. If she is afraid of dogs or can't tolerate their barking, do not get a dog! Most animals will be able to sense an autistic person's character, and will approach with care and patience. They will be able to sense intuitively if the child wants to engage in contact with them, yet is afraid. Animals have a certain energy that is quite soothing and relaxing for disabled people.

Small petting zoos are a lovely way to spend an afternoon with an autistic person who likes to be with animals. A visit to a farm also is a grand idea. Sheep, donkeys, and goats are friendly, soft creatures who easily come to little children and like to be offered pieces of carrot or apple. Large zoos can overwhelm an autistic, especially with their crowds of people and shouting youngsters. Autistic people like to touch and explore with hands and noses, so they should be given the opportunity to pet the animals which is not possible in most large, famous zoos.

There are some autistic children who are terrified of animals. There are also those who don't understand that they can cause pain to another creature so they torment small animals. Obviously, they must be kept away from animals, then, unless they learn how to not harm.

Some autistic people love swimming. It is a neat sensation to be under the water surface where everything sounds and looks beautifully bizarre. There are therapeutic swimming programmes involving dolphins. Dolphins are protective of people who have disabilities and will take great care to make sure the disabled one is safe. Dolphins have wit and charm and make superb playmates. For a fairly experienced autistic swimmer, one idea is scuba diving in tropical shallow water. The person will most likely tremendously enjoy the corals and being able to pet the colourful, unusual fish who glide by.

Going on holidays can be upsetting to the autistic child. Her schedule is disrupted. Staying in hotel rooms can be traumatic because everything is new, and the smells and sights are unfamiliar. There is a specific smell that is present in most hotel rooms, and it is irritating and cloying. Routines can be portable, however. The child can be comforted by transporting her own rituals from home, or by trying to substitute some of them with other similar items. Substitution sometimes doesn't work, though. Somebody must explain to the child before going on the holiday what is planned and that things will be different from things at home. Strategies can be discussed before hand. That autistic person should be able to enjoy the trip, also. It is best to keep trips mostly calm and peaceful, involving only the people the child is accustomed to living with.

There are autistic people who like to explore. So visiting different places can be stimulating. It's comforting for the person to bring along whatever objects she is attached to at home. Autistic people find comfort in various ways. Use whatever works. If the child is able to, let her pick some of the itinerary. As with any child, you can't expect an autistic person to always be patient, whilst you spend time doing something he doesn't have any interest in. Actually, in autistic people, this becomes harder because they don't want to spend time doing an activity they don't care anything about. Interest, of course, varies with the individual. Some youngsters have a focus and interest well beyond their years in certain things that non-autistic children would be terribly bored with, such as clocks. So that particular child might like to visit an antique clock museum.

Many children with Autism are an intriguing paradox of amazing seriousness and naivety, and emotional immaturity. Those traits don't necessarily have to clash in all instances. Since autistic people are so good at focusing, parents can use that trait to an advantage. If the child likes to draw, bring along a lot of paper and set him drawing so he doesn't get bored. That can also apply to books and to the child's beloved favourite comfort object. Autistic children can usually block out the surrounding environment during the times they're engaged in a preferred activity, even if the activity is merely sitting and rocking to and fro, or pacing a pattern on the carpet.

Going on a long tour isn't the best idea because too many changes are involved. Going from one hotel to another doesn't allow the autistic person enough time to get used to any of them. Close contact with strangers will probably traumatize the person, too. It's much more relaxing to go on a shorter holiday in a calm setting and stay in one hotel. Also, do try to travel in a car the child is familiar with.

Travel by train, jet, or ship may be devastating. Again, the environment all is new and there are many, many strangers all around. It can be confusing to the autistic youngster to be trapped in an unknown place surrounded by all new simulations. There are also people with Autism who enjoy travelling because they like to look at exciting things. They, too, still need to be grounded in their own rituals. They shouldn't merely be dragged along on holidays because they can't stay home by themselves (actually, some of them can). They can get enjoyment or education out of visiting other cities, and nations. Short simple trips make a good start to find out how the person can handle it.

Some autistic people are very interested in geography and looking at maps. They will enjoy visiting science museums or looking at antique maps. Even some very young autistic children read maps very well. They can help chart the travelling routes on long drives. Small, helpful tasks like that can be very exciting for them.

Do take advantage of the child's personal interests when travelling and visiting places. Many savants know information far beyond their years in their favourite subjects. They can help teach siblings and other family members and friends. Using their exceptional memories, they can share the new information from their sightseeing with the rest of the family. Here are some more suggestions for taking autistic people out to recreation spots, and for playtime at home:

1. For the child who is intensely interested in astronomy, take her to a local planetarium where she can sit beneath maps of stars projected above. That makes her obsession come alive instead of only looking at galaxies in textbooks, or trying to spot elusive planets on cloudy evenings. Consider buying her a good quality telescope that will reward her years of stargazing. Paint planets on her walls at home and construct a mobile of the solar system to suspend from her ceiling. If she is highly gifted, check into enrolling her in advanced astronomy courses in colleges. (This serves two purposes: furthering the child's knowledge on an advanced level, and helping regular college students to understand and know an autistic person first-hand!) College is mentioned here because beginning astronomy classes for children will bore the autistic who has acquired extensive knowledge on her own.

2. Computers! autistics love computers. They can tap in to learn about things they're interested in, and can even create their own programmes and contact other autistic people through the Internet.

3. If a child likes to look at tools, take him to a hardware shop. Buy him some kiddie tools to bang away with at home. Buy him some Lego sets. Only don't always expect him to construct a skyscraper with them. Instead, he may line them up into colour coded rows!

4. If the child likes to collect things, take advantage of that. If she likes rocks, take her to a science museum. Take her

digging to locate various types of rock. If she likes seashells, visit beaches and buy her several good books with photographs of international species of shells. If she likes marbles, begin a collection. Visit antique shops to search for unusual ones. Help her to shop for a fancy box to store them in. When travelling, pick up a few marbles as mementos of each place visited. That will mean more to the child than local souvenirs or an album of photographs. No matter what the child collects, show interest, even if it is something a bit unusual, such as pieces of velvet. The child has private reasons for collecting certain items, and they may not be able to be articulated.

5. If a child likes road signs, tell him to read aloud each sign as you pass by in the car. It will help to keep him interested, and make him feel he is being helpful.

6. For the music-loving child, provide him with an instrument. Wait to see how he teaches himself before getting a music teacher. Sometimes formal instruction removes an autistic person's interest. They can become confused by an outsider trying to tell them the way to do something while they've been getting the same results by their own methods. They also generally prefer solitary activities, and may fall apart in an ensemble situation.

7. Take the child to concerts and art museums if he is creative and able to sit quietly.

8. Depending upon the child's personality, take him to a crafts class. He may do better with other adults rather than in a class full of noisy non-autistic children. Since autistic people like to touch things, they can develop creative expression by doing macramé, origami, or putting model cars together. Many autistic children have exceptional fine motor capabilities and delicate, dextrous fingers.

9. If the child tolerates it, get her carefully involved in a synagogue, temple, or church youth organization. Some autistics who love to sing enjoy participating in a choir.

Often, however, a strictly social group is not going to interest an autistic boy or girl.

10. Bake something fun in the kitchen.

No child should be forced to participate in any activity she hates. It serves no purpose and only angers and upsets the child.

You can't expect the child with Autism to behave like non-autistic children, including in recreation. Much of the time, autistic people enjoy different things than others, or in different ways. That statement is closer to truth than to say they don't enjoy much at all. They frequently get something unexpected out of a certain activity. For their own reasons, they will return to it again and again. Of course enjoyment and feelings of fun in one who is autistic is the same as in any person. It's only the private path to arrive at particular emotions that varies for individuals.

Autistic people do have needs and wants like others have. They need to be loved deeply, they need to feel secure, they want to have fun, they want to play. Actually the differences are no greater than those between two non-autistic people; one whose recreation is sailing, and one whose recreation is playing chess. Both are quite dissimilar. Yet both make somebody feel good, or refreshed, or relaxed, or joyous, or free. Probably the surface appearances of deeply immersed autistics make them stand out. As they get their enjoyment from things that others don't find enjoyable, they seem so starkly unusual, perhaps shocking. Hopefully, as people become more educated about Autism, they won't be considered quite so odd. Perhaps the fear of something out-of-the-ordinary will be diminished, allowing people to be as different and extraordinary as they naturally are.

§

THIRTEEN

Idiosyncrasies and Special Traits

People with Autism have a great many idiosyncrasies. Some of them are funny. There are too many to mention them all, because they vary with the individual. They are an honest expression of each personality. Remember that, just as most other people think they are eccentric actions, the autistic doesn't think they are. He thinks everyone else is weird, and quite a puzzle.

Idiosyncratic behaviour often goes along with rituals. Autistic children and adults may ask a series of questions that are the same every day at the same time. They simply reassure him that things are proceeding as he feels they should. Questions are not intended to annoy anybody.

All ritualistic behaviour is for reassurance and creating order in daily life. Autistic people count on their routines. They give structure to the day. Specific rituals involving getting dressed each morning, or preparing for a task, may be quite long and complicated. Often, eating also becomes a ritual. Certain foods are eaten in certain ways, using the same progressive steps. Rituals are soothing and they do feel nice. They define areas of living. Religions have many rituals. Some of those are complicated, too. Routines and rituals just are a part of a person. Self-stimulations become part of the rituals, also.

Some autistic youngsters avoid stepping on their shadows and cracks in the pavement. They have their own private reasons for that. Usually, they're fairly bothered by the interruption of the crack intersecting smooth pavement. Sometimes they aren't sure that their shadow is a part of them. It seems like a separate being because it moves and comes very close to them, and touches them.

Since autistic people don't have much social sense, amusing things can occur in the midst of others. One autistic young man was preparing for bed and he couldn't locate his pyjamas. Downstairs his parents were entertaining dinner guests. So he wandered down, naked, to ask his mother where she'd put his pyjamas.

Another much younger lad loved water and to swim. One morning in the family's church, he spied the font where the people were blessing themselves with the holy water. He zipped over, before his mother had a chance to stop him and plunged his face in, and began blowing bubbles.

Often autistic people laugh at things only they know inside themselves. They get very joyful with the particular self-stimulation they're involved in, or they run funny mind movies in their heads. That helps a lot in scary or sad situations. Since their memories are so vivid, they just recall a scene they thought was funny in their past, and picture it all over again, exactly as it happened, complete with colour and sound. They can fixate on a particular tiny detail and think it is riotously hilarious. There can be a great deal of joy in an autistic's world.

It is true that non-conformists experience less stress. They don't care about fitting in. They don't waste energy striving to be like everybody else. They don't bring on strokes and heart attacks by constantly fretting over whether their every move is socially correct. Who really gives a damn? If you can feel happy and gentle towards yourself, that is so much more fulfilling than stifling your own emotions and desires just to be acceptable to other people.

Autism is certainly one of the types of non-conformity that comes naturally. Too much of the so-called treatments of Autism centre upon trying to strip all traces of the condition away. If that were possible – which it isn't – there would be only a shell left. The essence of the person would be removed. Then only a puppet would remain, a puppet trained to eat, sleep, act, dress, dance, laugh, and think like everybody else. Free countries have no right to allow governments to dictate a banishment of individuality. They penalize handicapped and different people, and they discriminate against them by either refusing to give them federal disability, or by begrudgingly surrendering a hideously tiny amount, way below poverty level, thereby ensuring the disabled one is unable to fulfil her potential. Meanwhile, they are generally trying to destroy the disabled person's privacy and they are making the person look like an idiot, and treating her like a criminal. That shows that they do not care, and do not want to help. That attitude leads the hostile indifference of the general public to anyone who doesn't conform.

Autistics are a lot better off, if they don't conform. Their idiosyncrasies are part of their badge of individuality. They don't go about trying to force everybody to act like they do. They mind their own business. They stand out but not in a vicious or dangerous way.

As they move about the house, often they tap objects. That is partly self-stimulatory, partly ritual, partly acknowledging an object's existence. They sometimes also follow certain family members around like a dog, from room to room. That definitely is not avoidance behaviour. As mentioned in a previous chapter, autistic people can be quite affectionate. Their ways of showing affection tend to be noticeable simply because they stray from the norm. They don't try to be pesty. They can be rather clingy. That is just a way to show they like someone.

It's as fun to laugh with an autistic child as it is to laugh with a non-autistic child. Often autistic little ones like to tumble about giggling hysterically. They may like being tickled by someone they trust.

Frequently autistic children burst out with a very funny statement. They are exceedingly honest and they say what they feel. They can be very generous to other people. They are deeply emotional and can be unusually compassionate. Although they are quite capable of caring about others, their outward expressions of caring differ from what is normally expected. They are very often misjudged as a result. This is not their fault, but is the mistake of regular people of society who don't attempt the insight to look with more than eyes.

Autism is not a terrifying, crippling disease. It is, of course, not an illness at all. Nothing is *wrong* with a person who was simply born autistic. There is only something *unique*. A different function of the brain doesn't mean that brain is damaged or incomplete. I fail to comprehend or accept how a great number of medical professionals, researchers, and even parents wish to eliminate a particular personality type, to stamp out something that makes some rare individuals stand out wonderfully from the crowds. How could I accept it? If their plan succeeded, I wouldn't be who I am. I suggest they spend their time and research funds on trying to find cures of the conditions that can kill, maim, or strip an individual of his dignity or desire to live, such as cancer and AIDS.

If every human being on this globe were the same, fitting perfectly into a master mold, what a boring world this would be!

A loving father or mother is proud of a child just for being who she or he is. It should not matter if the child never becomes a trillionaire, or famous politician. A parent can love and feel pride for a son or daughter who is a loving, sensitive, unique person, and who doesn't go about harming others. Being close to an individual with Autism is about celebrating life. It's about finding beauty in small things. It's about overcoming society's stigmas. It's about learning fresh ways to look at things. It does not have to be about tragedy or pain or loss. Bearing an autistic child is not losing that child. It's gaining a very special new son or daughter.

Autistics see things accurately. They have no delusions, and actually are surreal observers. They experience events as they happen. They make truthful observations. They often notice things that others miss because of their ability to focus, zeroing in close. They are free of the clutter that renders most people unable to retain their purity. They are not so easily conditioned by the masses. Since the effects of Autism in a person are so global, it proves that it is indeed much more a distinct personality, rather than a dysfunction. The autistic world is set up by the individual according to his specific inner rules. Everything has a reason.

Autistics are basically the same both in private and in public. They are judged mercilessly by a society that accepts only one rigid way of seeing. Many books describe autistic thinking as rigid. Autistic people do hold tightly to their routines, obsessions, and need to control their environment to prevent upsets. None of those is cruel towards others. But the big world's thinking is what is rigid. People who are not autistic seem to refuse to be willing to see Autism as anything other than a dreadful condition. They get as little information on it as they can, then dismiss it. Their ignorance fuels their refusal to open their minds to innovative perceptions. They judge too hastily without learning enough, or trying to be appreciative of people who are special.

If many more non-autistic humans knew more about the real Autism, then I think that their rigid beliefs would change. Non-autistic people have no right to dominate autistic people.

Some people regard Autism as a processing failure. It is indeed true that autistics process information differently, sometimes erratically. There are discrepancies over which traits of Autism are sources or symptoms and secondary symptoms. For the purpose of caring for an autistic child, that isn't important. People who love those with Autism deal with everyday characteristics. They deal with a very real person before them who has many eccentricities, charms, and a lot of ways to perplex others. So, cause and effect isn't as important as getting to know the autistic person better to love her as much as possible.

Some eccentric behaviour is to attract attention. Autistic children need a lot of attention, although they like to be ignored, too! They are people of great paradox.

Some people describe autistics as being selfish because living a self-absorbed life is confused with not caring about anyone else. Being self-absorbed is nothing terrible. Being self-centred simply means you are the centre of your own life. Autistics are not meanly selfish or vicious towards others. They don't scheme to harm others. They can feel sad when someone close to them is sad. Yet they can't be expected to give of themselves the same way others can. They are absorbed and involved in themselves, and deeply concerned about their own comfort. They don't as easily know what someone else is feeling without being told. They don't purposely reject everyone. They use their complex inner system of keeping everything regulated so they will feel safe and comfortable. True selfish actions involve knowing another is hurting, yet deliberately making it worse, or turning away. That is not Autism.

Autistic people more often are simply not aware of the needs of others. They have a different outlook and perception. They are quite capable of doing something nice for another. They don't want to be the cause of someone else's unhappiness. It does no good to make a gigantic issue of an autistic person's self-absorption. It simply is a fact.

Besides there seem to be many big world people who are cruelly self-ish, which is beyond self-absorption.

Actually, autistic children and adults can be amazingly tolerant. They live through a lot of discrimination and abuse, without fighting back in many cases. When they develop their own voices and mode of communication and can stand up for themselves, then they usually surprise others. Autistic people see things as they are, so they are interestingly free of being brainwashed by other people. They have an innocence that helps them see beyond the mere colour of an individual's skin. They see prejudice as ridiculous. They can't comprehend why someone should be hated just for following a different religion, or for having a darker or lighter skin tone. They can easily recognize hate words, and they can feel deeply upset to see a person being bullied by others. Because they do see the truth as it is presented, they are overwhelmed by the stupidity and immorality of prejudice. They see the victim of discrimination just as he or she is. If they see a dark skinned Pakistani boy being tormented by a mob of white schoolmates, they will see the image as it truly is. They will see a boy who is being hurt by others for a very insignificant reason: he has darker skin than the rest.

That is essentially all that prejudice is. It is picking a very tiny part of a person – religion, skin colour, gender, romantic preference, weight – and then inflating it to define that person – as though that person had no other characteristics at all. Then the hate groups create their own definitions to fit along with the main trait that they feel makes another inferior. As an example, the hate groups (and members of the general public who are swayed by them) see a black man, so they attach a list of negative traits to him: he is black because a god made him inferior, or he is a thief and lazy, and he certainly must beat his wife, and he smells strange, etc. Or with a homosexual individual, they will say he is not 'normal,' he is a 'sinner', he is weak and disgusting and will go to 'hell', and they sneer at him and call him 'faggot'.

Autistic people understand the feeling of being oppressed. They see directly through all the lies created by those who are prejudiced. They are enraged by the way some individuals are treated, because they look at a person and see *a person* before they see that the person happens to be white, Japanese, or Jewish or a man or a woman, or slender, or obese.

Autistic grown-ups and teenagers can be very concerned about the environment because they can accept the fact that, when certain things are gone, they cannot be replaced. Youngsters with Autism can feel good about their contributions. They can participate in small tasks, such as bundling newspapers for the recycling, because many of them like chores, and want to feel they are important.

People with Autism need to know where they stand in relationships. They need to have reassurance of someone's love. If a parent gets angry and shouts, the child may interpret that as a sign that the parent doesn't love him. It's helpful to keep the voice soft and even. Once again, it is a desire for sameness that every autistic needs which is an influence. Some family member's anger eruption disturbs the equilibrium. Balance is of much importance in the autistic person's daily life.

Another trait of Autism is to get upset by another person coming into the house. That is another disruption of the daily routine. Autistic people are territorial, too. They see their house as an extension of themselves. If they live by themselves in their own homes, they generally can't bear the thought of anybody coming in. They surely get quite upset if the guest touches or moves any objects. The boundaries extend outward from the immediate body. So the person takes it personally, as though she is actually the one being touched. A guest in an autistic person's home should always ask if he might touch an item that interests him. That applies to everything, not only valuable objects. Autistics can grow very attached to their possessions, no matter what their apparent value.

A repair person entering the house is a big opportunity for the autistic to freak out. The person feels confused by the intruder because he or she doesn't live there or belong there. The arrival of a repair person must be as quiet as possible. It's best to explain a bit about the special child's possible reactions to prepare Mr. or Ms. Fix-it for any unusual behaviour. I think that sometimes autistic behaviour shocks strangers. The child may run up to the person and touch his equipment and sniff him, as a way to explore.

The child or grown-up should also be warned before the repair person arrives. Then, if the child permits it, she should be kept busy and safe in her room during the time the handy person is present. Some autistic children who are very interested in electronics and how things work may enjoy watching the repair as the plumber, electrician, or whoever, explains what he or she is doing. It's important to explain to the autistic person that the handy person is not here to harm or disrupt anything the child owns. Explain that the repair must be made so the family and the autistic may once again enjoy the pleasure of using what has broken.

Autistic children are very curious. If they're not being supervised, they may open other people's bags and begin peering through them. They can't translate their own aversion to having their own belongings fingered to other people. They don't fully realize that non-autistics may not want their belongings handled by an unknown strange child or adult. Autistic people have difficulty guessing the feelings or thoughts of others. When they are told of them, they remember, but it still may not make sense to them, because they are mostly so aware only of themselves. Facts can be remembered, but the subtle understanding of another's mind is missing.

The best thing is to get a child diagnosed as early as possible. Then the family can learn and understand while growing. It is extremely difficult for an older autistic person, who has an entire childhood of confusion and most likely pain from being tormented. Early diagnosis is not to be done to start the little one in therapy to become less autistic and to conform to other's ways. It is to help child and family to form a solid unit of love in the very early years of the autistic one's life. It is to help lessen the years of fear that can come later on. The growing autistic who doesn't know he's autistic hurts because he senses he is not like others, but has no idea why. Teachers can complain and urge parents to take their girl or boy to a doctor. Classmates can verbally tear apart the autistic youngster, which creates self-hatred, low self-esteem, and unimaginable hurt. Most autistics who are diagnosed when they are grown have a hard period of reliving a past of pain, as well as the possibility of resentment and a lot of trapped rage.

Some of that could have been avoided by taking the person to a good doctor or series of doctors when much younger. Becoming familiar with the term Autism and learning about it provides something real to hold on to. You can get reassurance to discover that something you do is characteristic of Autism. You can learn what it is that makes you strike out so much. Then you don't believe the others when they call you a freak because you know you're not. Now you can be proud of who you are.

There are autistics who enjoy being autistic. There are also those who don't. I think all do find some comfort in their personal worlds. They should not be compared to others. That is unfair and basically is not applicable. What somebody else has or does may never be possible for a particular autistic to have or do, which isn't a tragedy. People need to find their own paths to joy and peace. They can't follow someone else's exact path. The friends and family of an autistic can't say to that person, 'If you had what we have, you would be happy', since nobody truly knows that.

The basic ingredients of living in joy can be obtained and stirred by both autistic and non-autistic. Everyone has a right to be happy. Autism doesn't take away that right, nor does it prevent one from feeling happy. A physical brain difference need not be seen as a private hell, keeping its afflicted prisoners.

So, Autism can't be simply defined in a dictionary as 'one who is self-absorbed and lives in a fantasy world'. Autism is a many faceted, deeply intense personality type, and it deserves to be treated as such. It deserves to be nurtured and respected. It needs to be taught in schools. It does not deserve to be stamped out. People who have Autism are different and beautiful.

Many autistic people affectionately, humorously refer to themselves as aliens. They feel displaced on a vast planet, which has a code of life, and understanding they can't ever quite subscribe to. If they are welcomed, however, and cherished as the individuals they are, then there wouldn't be as much dissension on both sides. Aliens can become more comfortable and less paralyzed in fear, while still remaining who they are. Their essence stays the same. Then they don't have to despise their alien status, as if it were forced upon them. Instead, they can enjoy their uniqueness, just as others enjoy theirs.

HOME

A child encapsulated

Her inner world of music,
sensations luscious honey,
spicy-rich-warm cinnamon,
a sanctuary of soft movements.
   Rocking body,
    fingers floating before deep eyes,
    feet wandering soothing circles,
Serene in autistic quiet,
Serene eyes,
Serene hands,
Happy
Living in her simple coloured box,
Her blown-glass world,
Home
Self-enclosed dream child,
Toe-steps her own exotic rhythm,
She shields the egg of her universe
with wide wings.

§

For Autistic People

Autistic people seem to like to learn about one another. There is a tremendous curiosity about your fellow alien beings. It's intriguing to discover other unique people. It feels like a cosy comfort to get in touch with another who has a lot of your same experiences at the core. Since Autism is rather rare, many autistics grow up never meeting another person like them. They will find strength in contacting each other and discussing their experiences.

As an autistic girl, I would have 'my people' know that they each have a right to take pride in who they are. They don't deserve to suffer a lifetime of guilt because they didn't turn out the way other people thought they would. The sense of guilt is put upon them by others. There is a choice to get rid of guilt and move on. Autism need not be an enemy to you.

To the autistic reader, I have some tips. Find a support system. A few true friends will help you feel you are appreciated and loved. You must remember to love yourself, too. To be true to yourself is a way of loving yourself. Accepting your emotions and your sensitivities is also a way to be kind to yourself. Being born autistic is no reason to live in misery. You still can be gentle to yourself.

When nobody around you understands, it feels astonishingly lonely. The only place to go then is within yourself. You can be your own best friend. In forming friendships with others, they need to be honest and loving, or they are useless as true friends.

Lifetimes of pain can make you strong and lovely like a polished stone made smooth by buffeting water. The pain will not last forever. You, yourself, can help open the door to let pain go. You don't need the pain anymore, so why cling to it? Why allow it to take up space in your world? People who have Autism can be happy, too. You need to remember that the bad treatment from others is because they have a problem with you. You didn't make them have their problem. They caused themselves to have the problem. Rise above.

Picture yourself as a phoenix that dies in flames and is then resurrected fresh and shining. Go beyond the past so it can't continue to harm you. Don't keep punishing yourself by replaying your awful experiences. They are now only memories. Memories for us are vivid. So turn to happy memories then and imagine them blotting out the bad ones.

Someone with Autism can be free and joyous. Appreciating and liking yourself is liberating. Even if you don't really understand yourself you can be a friend to yourself. Write about your emotions and thoughts so you can see them in words. They form patterns of their own, just as your rituals do. Paint your emotional tidal waves! Sing them! Write them into poems!. View them as a beautiful part of creative you. If any outsider complains about your precious emotions, you need to remain strong. Be free. If you must laugh, then laugh. If you must cry, then cry. Autistics need space to develop and know themselves. Express yourself.

Be the real you. Try to not mimic others because the real you is more important. You can still feel safest way deep in you even if you don't pretend to become someone else. You have your own uniqueness. You have opinions and desires that are worthwhile.

If you want to do something, try to do it. Seize your own day. Let no one crush your dreams. You don't have to follow others' way of doing things because you have your own life. If you need some special help from anyone, do not be ashamed. If you are confused, do not be embarrassed. Your honesty is still better than mimicking others and getting perplexed as to where the real you begins.

It's often excruciating to have others directly acknowledge you. Your existence proves you are a separate self and don't literally disappear as you try to do. No matter how withdrawn you are, you still have a self. Acknowledging that you have opinions and dreams proves you have a self, an individual spirit, complete with separate personality. There can be a fear of revealing any of your own beliefs because someone else may disagree or even condemn. Then you grow to expect that all others think you're an idiot. You can grow frightened into silence. You need instead to stand up to them. Everyone has a right to a belief system, complete with opinions.

You need to discover who you really are, and celebrate that. If others don't totally agree with you, then that's simply going to be the way it is. Don't compromise yourself for them. Don't punish yourself with self-depreciation merely because someone else doesn't share the same opinions. Youll always have your inner sanctum.

Succumbing to the masses is a crime of communization. Everybody is *not* the same. Going along with others just to avoid getting condemned is apathy. Apathy is what caused Adolph Hitler to gain such tremendous power in the early years of the developing Reich. Apathy is what caused the racial injustices that went on until Martin Luther King Jr. stood up and organized a movement of civil rights. Apathy can destroy an individual, a group, and a nation. It stinks to be laughed at and called mean names every day. But I think it stinks more to allow them to win by taking away your spirit, and igniting a spark of self-hatred deep inside you.

There are many people who respect and appreciate autistic people. There are many people who don't enjoy hurting others. You must locate a few of them so you don't have to face pain all alone. It's quite true that our Autism generates a type of isolation. That can be good. Only when you face an enemy it's no good to be all alone. You will have more strength if you have even a tiny support group to be your friends.

You can fulfil dreams. Just because you may need more help than others doesn't mean you can't achieve dreams. You can have someone close to you who takes care of you in some ways, and still be happy. Nothing is wrong with leaning on a friend. If you think there is a point of your Autism that is negative, you can try to change it. The best self-help is to realize Autism is a gift and not meant to cause anguish to you or others. It's not an excuse for abuse.

You must find your own wee niche in life. You deserve to be happy. You need to find your own way to be happy. You need not spend a fortune of money on a psychiatrist to 'fix' you. You don't need to be fixed. You aren't broken. If you can find a therapist or counsellor you trust to help you through times that are uncomfortable, then you can have another friend in that person. He or she should have a thorough knowledge of Autism and not just be a regular psychologist or teacher. Autism causes many things to affect a person differently than from a non-autistic person, so a good professional will understand that.

It is okay to feel things deeply. It is okay to be you. I do hope that you will be able to discover yourself as you learn and grow. I hope you can celebrate who you are, and feel strong in your simplicity and purity. Inside you in a very deep place, can live a universe. You can see yourself as a multi-faceted stained glass window. Think of your life as bursting with radiating intense moods and colours. Your life can be a rainbow.

THE END

§

Poems

Jasmine

Little jasmine bloom
Wind-tossed to me
Nestled on my cheek
Wet with rain,
Over the mountain comes thunder,
A breeze no stronger than you
Whisks you suddenly away again.

Rain

He said 'I am the Rain.'
I ran to him
through wet reeds,
cat-o-nine tails rapping my shins,
The water droplets sang
as we grew together to stand
before the sun.

Casey

As autumn winds toss trees,
I roll from bed to smile at
my wee rust and black-striped friend,
rescued from a car-worn street,
Body bent into a question mark,
Casey munches a leaf of mustard,
typewriter neat,
My curious fuzzy fellow
hurries up his twig,
waves his upper body in air,
sets tiny sticky feet onto my offered finger,
marches nimbly up my thigh,
pushing his head into a trouser fold,
he shyly coils into a ball,
I gently tumble him back into his jar home,
He rests beneath his greenery
to gather energy for his important spin,
When caterpillar fuzz will turn into silken wings.

Samurai Widow

Heaven spurned
millions, millions of snowdrop tears
blooming on his shining cloak
slumped in a pile
with his crest of a dragon's head,
No son to press it
against his cheeks and let
the dragon lick his tears,
Widow walks like a statue
A windy palace all her own,
She stepstepsteps barefoot,
orders the maids away,
Her hair
unshackled in silken sheaves
like dragon's mane.

The waiting maid's song
a lonely thrush,
Widow kneels in dim Shinto light,
shadows creep, dart, snake,
glint off steel,
One flash,
No tears,
Widow's final note is silence,
Her dagger through her throat,
Maid's song fades into bamboo whisper,
Yards and yards of snowdrop silk
crumple and turn scarlet

Tango

A scent of lily-of-the-valley
on a current of musical air,
he turns his angled chin,
brown velvet eyes
curl their wings around her

Lone woman folded,
at her table,
lithe figure hugged in jade silk,
solitary shepherd of lost wishes,
She, so lovely that stars gasp in their orbits,
The world is born and dies in her.
She crosses legs of elegance,
clutches dainty hands together,
Shadows skip across her bare back
bolted straight with shyness

He hears the rustle of jade silk
louder than the beat of jazz,
He brushes unseen dust from his pinstripes,
steps softly to her,
she lifts gold-nugget eyes,
her hand rests in his palm

They swirl away to a tango,
his skin sighing at her closeness,
He wonders if she can see
the loneliness,
asks himself if she can know
that his penthouse is too vast for him alone.
The way her body molds to him
tells him she thinks he's handsome,
with gentleman's grace,
fingertips on her petite back,
he guides her round the dance floor,
already breathing with her
Eyes closed in rhythm
he whispers in her ear,
she answers,
her breath a breeze of peppermint,
his chin brushes her brow,
damp with flushed joy

Her heartbeat bounds at his infant-soft touch,
–Maybe, maybe, he is for me,
He smiles
at how perfect is her tiny hand in his,
–Maybe, maybe, she is for me.

For Joseph M.

(Joseph Merrick, who was called The Elephant Man)

As specks of sand scatter in the wind,
Your memory scatters and fades,
Your image preserved in medical books,
While most hearts never know you.

Soft soul, delicate, nestled within a hated body,
barnacled, tumoured, enlarged but for
      a small, perfect left arm and hand,
       beautiful as an artist's,
and gentle dark eyes.
With the head of a giant and a limping hip,
You moved drenched in cloak and cap
to seclude you from stabbing eyes,
You were diminutive, yet enormous,
and they called you Elephant Man,
Abandoned into Victorian squalour
to become circus treasure
      was the only path open to you,
Fear of crowds' screams of revulsion and sneers
      tired your tender spirit
      encased in the body of a bizarre apparition,
With your crazy-shaped shadow
hidden until your carnival master
      flourished the curtain aside,
The masses' horror stares
      banished you
to be the silent idiot they thought you to be
When your saviour came,
He found you scrunched in a heap of quiet loss,
That kind doctor who gave you respite
seemed to you an angel,
When you shyly spoke to him
he was stricken by your wit and
the vastness of the bright mind that glowed from you,

Charming as the song bird,
Loving as a mediaeval virgin,
for you WERE beautiful.
Sudden life exploded for you,
In wonder, every day
brought tiny miracles,
Simple beauty
          was hidden in years of fear,
In romantic innocence,
You adored pretty women,
Picked flowers from the meadows,
Joyfully read towers of books,
Your new family multiplied,
          Doctor, actress, duke, princess,
their photographs filled your room with smiles,
You cherished each one with child awe,
To them you needn't fear
          showing your unmasked face,
your one beloved prize,
An elegant dressing box, barely usable,
Your distorted face couldn't be shaved,
Your several thin hairs needed no brushing,
But, every day, you arranged
          silver shining combs, brushes, cigarette case,
And, in imagination,
became a dandy who drew only admiration.
You longed to sleep like others,
rather than propped into a triangle,
But the weight of your swollen head would crush your air,
Still, one night, you tried,
you melted into bed,
          your giant head sank,
          they found you later, suffocated

You, extraordinary mortal,
Formed of uncommon flesh and courage,
You can teach true beauty.

For Dr. R

When you look ar me
with sea-pale eyes,
my pain sails away,
when you're not watching
I peek your way,
My snow-bearded friend,
I love you.

I, snug in a ball
in your arms rocking me,
I call you Daddy in dreams,
Wonderful creative healer,
Thoughts always tickled by your face
and your soft murmurs,
My mornings with you
are like treasures like rosy seashells,
you help unlock my big love
bursting me,
you love me as I am,
in my own stained glass world

Further Reading

Nobody Nowhere
by Donna Williams
This is an autobiography of a marvellous young autistic woman. It has helped many autistic adults finally realize what it is that makes them different.

Autism: An Inside-Out Approach
by Donna Williams
This is a thorough informative text dealing with the many, many aspects of Autism and how to deal with them. Its emphasis is on understanding people with Autism, and what is going on within them. It is deeply insightful.

Autism: Explaining the Enigma
by Uta Frith
This goes beyond the archaic theories into innovative explanations on Autism. It is fascinating to read and full of many truths.

Talking in Pictures
by Temple Grandin
Here is another autistic autobiography, which is also a kind of thesis containing general information on Autism.

Russell is Extra Special
by Charles A. Amenta, III, M.D.
This is a book for children. The author's beautiful son, Russell, has Autism. It is illustrated with lovely family-oriented photographs that are not stilted or posed. The feeling of the story is not negative, but rather respectful and loving. It is excellent for helping little ones learn about special people.

Andy and His Yellow Frisbee
by Mary Thompson
Another book for children. It is wonderfully illustrated by the author. It explains a bit about Autism facts. Even better, though, is its message of patience and gentleness when dealing with autistic children.

An Anthropologist on Mars
by Oliver Sacks, M.D.

This doesn't deal only with Autism. There is a long chapter on Temple Grandin, however, and one dealing with savants, most of whom are autistic. It is written about various unusual types of people, and its message is respect for those who are extraordinary.

Detecting Your Hidden Allergies
by William Crook, M.D.
This is helpful for those who suspect they have specific food allergies.

Neurobiological Issues in Autism
edited by Eric Schopler and Gary Mesibov
One of a series of medical texts called 'Current Issues in Autism'. Eric Schopler and Gary Mesibov are the founders of the TEACCH (Treatment and Education of autistic and related Communication handicapped Children) method for all ages of autistic people. This book goes into a lot of detail about the specific brain differences of autistic individuals.

High-Functioning Individuals with Autism
edited by Eric Schopler and Gary Mesibov
Another in the 'Current Issues in Autism' series. This book is filled with fascinating, engaging portraits of more able autistic people.

The Child's Conception of the World
by Jean Paiget
Here is a classic of child psychology. For readers who are interested in extensively studying Autism, it's helpful to study psychology in general. Traits of Autism are better understood when they are applied and contrasted with non-autistic behaviour.

Index

12889458R00082

Made in the USA
Lexington, KY
07 January 2012